Ethics

Other Books in the Current Controversies Series:

Ethics

Brenda Stalcup, *Book Editor*

David Bender, *Publisher*
Bruno Leone, *Executive Editor*

Bonnie Szumski, *Editorial Director*
David M. Haugen, *Managing Editor*

CURRENT CONTROVERSIES

Cover photo: C.J. Gunter/Sipa Press

Library of Congress Cataloging-in-Publication Data

Ethics / Brenda Stalcup, book editor.
    p. cm. — (Current controversies)
    Includes bibliographical references and index.
    ISBN 0-7377-0338-5 (lib. : alk. paper). — ISBN 0-7377-0337-7
(pbk. : alk. paper)
    1. Ethics. I. Stalcup, Brenda. II. Series.

BJ1012 .E8865   2000
170—dc21   99-045248
                                                                    CIP

©2000 by Greenhaven Press, Inc., PO Box 289009, San Diego, CA 92198-9009
Printed in the U.S.A.

Contents

No: American Business Is Becoming Less Ethical

Yes: American Business Is Becoming More Ethical

Chapter 3: Are Modern Biomedical Practices Ethical?

Yes: Modern Biomedical Practices Are Ethical

Cloning techniques have the potential to be used in the treatment or cure
of many diseases, including life-threatening illnesses such as cancer. The
cloning of humans could also be beneficial in a variety of ways. Cloning
is not an unethical practice; in fact, banning research into the possible
benefits of cloning is itself unethical.

Stem cells can develop into any organ or tissue in the human body;
research into stem cells may provide new treatments for cancer, diabetes,
and other serious medical problems. Because stem cells are collected
from human embryos, many people believe the research is unethical.
However, stem cells are taken from surplus embryos created for in vitro
fertilization that will be destroyed whether or not they are used for
research. Federal funding of stem cell research will ensure that it continues to be conducted in an ethical manner.

Because there is a chronic shortage of human organs donated for transplants, many patients die while waiting for organs to become available.
Allowing people to sell their organs or otherwise compensating them
could go a long way toward solving this problem. In most cases, people
would agree to allow their organs to be harvested after their death in
return for financial compensation to their survivors.

No: Modern Biomedical Practices Are Unethical

As the prospect of human cloning becomes increasingly more feasible,
society should take steps to prevent it. Early experiments with human
cloning would undoubtedly prove harmful to most of the cloned children.
Furthermore, cloning would irrevocably damage the sanctity and dignity
of human life.

Stem cell research may result in promising medical advances, but utilizing stem cells from human embryos is unethical despite any beneficial
outcome. New scientific advances into other, more ethical sources of
human stem cells should be pursued, while any stem cell research that
requires the destruction of human embryos should be banned.

Although there is a critical shortage of human organs available for transplantation, allowing people to sell their organs on an open market is not
an ethical solution to this problem. Donating an organ is an irrevocable
and medically risky option, but many people would be so tempted by the

prospect of financial gain that they would not fully consider the consequences of their decision.

Chapter 4: How Can Ethical Behavior Be Taught?

Foreword

By definition, controversies are "discussions of questions in which opposing opinions clash" (Webster's Twentieth Century Dictionary Unabridged). Few would deny that controversies are a pervasive part of the human condition and exist on virtually every level of human enterprise. Controversies transpire between individuals and among groups, within nations and between nations. Controversies supply the grist necessary for progress by providing challenges and challengers to the status quo. They also create atmospheres where strife and warfare can flourish. A world without controversies would be a peaceful world; but it also would be, by and large, static and prosaic.

The Series' Purpose

The purpose of the Current Controversies series is to explore many of the social, political, and economic controversies dominating the national and international scenes today. Titles selected for inclusion in the series are highly focused and specific. For example, from the larger category of criminal justice, Current Controversies deals with specific topics such as police brutality, gun control, white collar crime, and others. The debates in Current Controversies also are presented in a useful, timeless fashion. Articles and book excerpts included in each title are selected if they contribute valuable, long-range ideas to the overall debate. And wherever possible, current information is enhanced with historical documents and other relevant materials. Thus, while individual titles are current in focus, every effort is made to ensure that they will not become quickly outdated. Books in the Current Controversies series will remain important resources for librarians, teachers, and students for many years.

In addition to keeping the titles focused and specific, great care is taken in the editorial format of each book in the series. Book introductions and chapter prefaces are offered to provide background material for readers. Chapters are organized around several key questions that are answered with diverse opinions representing all points on the political spectrum. Materials in each chapter include opinions in which authors clearly disagree as well as alternative opinions in which authors may agree on a broader issue but disagree on the possible solutions. In this way, the content of each volume in Current Controversies mirrors the mosaic of opinions encountered in society. Readers will quickly realize that there are many viable answers to these complex issues. By questioning each author's conclusions, students and casual readers can begin to develop the critical thinking skills so important to evaluating opinionated material.

Current Controversies is also ideal for controlled research. Each anthology in the series is composed of primary sources taken from a wide gamut of informational categories including periodicals, newspapers, books, United States and foreign government documents, and the publications of private and public organizations. Readers will find factual support for reports, debates, and research papers covering all areas of important issues. In addition, an annotated table of contents, an index, a book and periodical bibliography, and a list of organizations to contact are included in each book to expedite further research.

Perhaps more than ever before in history, people are confronted with diverse and contradictory information. During the Persian Gulf War, for example, the public was not only treated to minute-to-minute coverage of the war, it was also inundated with critiques of the coverage and countless analyses of the factors motivating U.S. involvement. Being able to sort through the plethora of opinions accompanying today's major issues, and to draw one's own conclusions, can be a complicated and frustrating struggle. It is the editors' hope that Current Controversies will help readers with this struggle.

Greenhaven Press anthologies primarily consist of previously published material taken from a variety of sources, including periodicals, books, scholarly journals, newspapers, government documents, and position papers from private and public organizations. These original sources are often edited for length and to ensure their accessibility for a young adult audience. The anthology editors also change the original titles of these works in order to clearly present the main thesis of each viewpoint and to explicitly indicate the opinion presented in the viewpoint. These alterations are made in consideration of both the reading and comprehension levels of a young adult audience. Every effort is made to ensure that Greenhaven Press accurately reflects the original intent of the authors included in this anthology.

"Regardless of whether or not ethical standards have declined overall, . . . ethics is still an important matter of concern in the United States."

Introduction

In 1999, the world watched in shock and dismay as President Bill Clinton underwent an impeachment trial for lying under oath about his extramarital affair with White House intern Monica Lewinsky. Although Clinton was ultimately acquitted of charges of high crimes and misdemeanors, he did admit to the relationship and his attempts to cover it up.

Many critics point to Clinton's actions as indicative of a severe lack of ethics in America. They insist that modern Americans are far less ethical than previous generations and more willing to accept unethical behavior in their leaders. According to other commentators, however, the notion that Americans were more ethical in years past is simply a myth. For example, they argue, among former presidents, Franklin D. Roosevelt continued to have an affair after promising his wife he would end the relationship, and recent scientific evidence has strongly indicated that Thomas Jefferson fathered at least one child with his slave Sally Hemmings. While not condoning unethical behavior, these commentators express the view that the present generation of Americans is not unique in sometimes failing to live up to its own high standards.

Regardless of whether or not ethical standards have declined overall, the controversy over Clinton's behavior demonstrates that ethics is still an important matter of concern in the United States. Most Americans believe that society operates more smoothly if people adhere to certain core values and do not lie, cheat, or steal. They would prefer for their leaders, coworkers, and neighbors to be honest, fair, considerate, and trustworthy. Perhaps most of all, they want their children to learn these values and to grow up to be ethical adults.

In recent years, as concern over the ethical standards of Americans has risen, more and more parents and politicians have called for the schools to help educate children in good moral values. According to Merrilee A. Boyack, an attorney and parent in California who supports teaching values in the schools,

> One of the primary functions of our educational system is to educate future citizens of our country and to properly instruct them in areas that will lead them to function well in that role. We cannot expect citizens to be law-abiding, responsible and charitable if we give them no such instruction.

In response to this call for the schools' involvement, a number of educators have promoted an approach known as character education. Character education

11

emphasizes the integration of moral and ethical issues into the curriculum. In a character education program, textbooks and other reading materials contain stories promoting courage, responsibility, and tolerance; classroom discussions often focus on finding solutions for ethical dilemmas. Ideally, every lesson and activity in the classroom should include a component designed to teach ethical behavior. Furthermore, teachers are expected to serve as good role models and to encourage their students to behave in an ethical manner.

Character education has been hailed by many as an innovative and successful method for instilling values in young students. These supporters maintain that students who are taught using character education techniques not only learn about ethics but also spontaneously begin to practice ethical behavior in their own lives. For example, advocates point to a long-term study that followed fifty children in Oakland, California, who were enrolled in an intensive character education program from kindergarten to eighth grade. When compared to their peers who had not had character education, these children evidenced better manners, friendlier dispositions, fewer discipline problems, and higher conflict-resolution skills. Noting such successes, Esther F. Schaeffer, the executive director of the Character Education Partnership, asserts that "character education belongs as an integral part of a child's education."

However, some educators and commentators question whether character education actually has a long-term impact on the behavior of children. Character education programs are relatively new, they point out; most have only been in existence since the mid- or late 1990s. It will take many more years of research to fully evaluate the effects of such programs, these commentators contend. Moreover, a number of educators are concerned that the expectations for character education are overly high. According to James Leming, a professor of education at Southern Illinois University, "If you read the rationale for character education, it says we have a drug problem, a crime problem, a sexual promiscuity problem, and if we'd only do character education in our schools, we could fix all these problems." Leming advocates a more realistic assessment of character education's potential, cautioning that "it's naive to expect teachers to . . . turn everyone into good little boys and girls by doing lessons in their classrooms." Thomas J. Lasley II, an education professor at the University of Dayton in Ohio, argues that children learn far more about values from the messages they receive from their parents, the media, and society. "In a culture in which . . . fewer people think beyond their individual needs," he argues, "it is doubtful that school programs [in character education] will prove successful if they seek to teach children the lessons that adults have not yet learned." Lasley and other critics insist that values education must be centered in the home, not in the school system, in order to succeed.

The role of educators in imparting values to children is only one of the debates surrounding the subject of ethics. As modern society grows more complex and diverse, questions concerning ethics continue to increase in importance, but they also appear to become more difficult to resolve. The authors included in *Ethics: Current Controversies* debate a variety of ethical issues and dilemmas in the following chapters: What Motivates People to Behave Ethically? Is American Business Becoming More Ethical? Are Modern Biomedical Practices Ethical? How Can Ethical Behavior Be Taught? The ethical questions raised in these chapters may not be easily answered, but their consideration is essential to maintaining and improving the moral fiber of society.

Chapter 1

What Motivates People to Behave Ethically?

Chapter Preface

For centuries, philosophers, theologians, and other scholars have attempted to determine what factors motivate people to act ethically. Religion has frequently been cited as a primary force motivating ethical behavior. All religions contain specific ethical principles that believers are expected to follow. People may follow the ethical guidelines of their religion through fear of divine punishment if they transgress or in anticipation of being rewarded for leading a virtuous life.

Recently, however, some scientists have proposed that humans' sense of ethical behavior evolved through natural selection. They maintain that an individual's altruistic behavior, such as warning relatives of the approach of dangerous animals, increased the likelihood that these early humans would survive the threat and would live to pass on their altruistic genes to their descendants. According to this theory, humans are "hardwired" for ethical behavior.

The idea that humans may be biologically predisposed to ethical behavior is disturbing to many theologians and religious individuals. Even some scientists find the proposition unsettling, as Randolph Neese confesses: "The discovery that tendencies to altruism are shaped by benefits to genes is one of the most disturbing in the history of science. When I first grasped it, I slept badly for many nights, trying to find some alternative that did not so roughly challenge my sense of good and evil." According to author John Maynard Smith,

> Is there any way in which we can decide, with certainty, which actions are right? [There] is not, unless you hold that . . . human beings are here to do God's bidding. If a person is simply the product of his or her genetic makeup and environmental history, . . . there is simply no source whence absolute morality could come.

However, others assert that this scientific theory can be compatible with religious belief. For example, Christian author Larry Arnhart insists, "If God is the all-powerful and all-good Creator of nature, then there is no reason to believe that the natural constitution of human beings has been designed in opposition to moral goodness." According to this view, ethical behavior is motivated by a biological imperative that was given to humans by a divine creator.

Understanding the motivations behind ethical behavior is not simply a philosophical debate: These theories can influence society to adopt certain measures to encourage ethical behavior or to address chronic unethical behavior in individuals such as criminals. The contributors to the following chapter debate the answer to the lingering question of what causes humans to act ethically.

Belief in God Motivates People to Behave Ethically

by Benedict de Spinoza

About the author: *Benedict de Spinoza (1632–1677) was a Dutch philosopher. Born a Sephardic Jew, as a young man he was excommunicated from the Jewish community for his thoughts and practices. Spinoza proposed that people are guided by their own natures, and that virtuous people understand their own na-tures and ultimately seek to understand the nature of God. Spinoza wrote the books* A Treatise on Religious and Political Philosophy, Political Treatise, *and* Ethics, *from which this viewpoint is excerpted.*

I should like to say a few words about perfection and imperfection, and about good and evil. If a man has proposed to do a thing and has accomplished it, he calls it perfect, and not only he, but every one else who has really known or has believed that he has known the mind and intention of the author of that work will call it perfect too. For example, having seen some work (which I suppose to be as yet not finished), if we know that the intention of the author of that work is to build a house, we shall call the house imperfect; while, on the other hand, we shall call it perfect as soon as we see the work has been brought to the end which the author had determined for it. But if we see any work such as we have never seen before, and if we do not know the mind of the workman, we shall then not be able to say whether the work is perfect or imperfect. This seems to have been the first signification of these words; but afterwards men began to form universal ideas, to think out for themselves types of houses, buildings, castles, and to prefer some types of things to others; and so it hap-pened that each person called a thing perfect which seemed to agree with the universal idea which he had formed of that thing, and, on the other hand, he called a thing imperfect which seemed to agree less with his typical conception, although, according to the intention of the workman, it had been entirely com-

Benedict de Spinoza, from *The Ethics of Spinoza*, translated by W.H. White and revised by A.H. Stirling. Reprinted by permission of Oxford University Press.

pleted. This appears to be the only reason why the words *perfect* and *imperfect* are commonly applied to natural objects which are not made with human hands; for men are in the habit of forming, both of natural as well as of artificial objects, universal ideas which they regard as types of things, and which they think nature has in view, setting them before herself as types too; it being the common opinion that she does nothing except for the sake of some end. When, therefore, men see something done by nature which does not altogether answer to that typal conception which they have of the thing, they think that nature herself has failed or committed an error, and that she has left the thing imperfect. Thus we see that the custom of applying the words *perfect* and *imperfect* to natural objects has arisen rather from prejudice than from true knowledge of them. For . . . nature does nothing for the sake of an end, for that eternal and infinite Being whom we call God or Nature acts by the same necessity by which He exists; . . . He acts by the same necessity of nature as that by which He exists. The reason or cause, therefore, why God or nature acts and the reason why He exists are one and the same. Since, therefore, He exists for no end, He acts for no end; and since He has no principle or end of existence, He has no principle or end of action. A final cause, as it is called, is nothing, therefore, but human desire, in so far as this is considered as the principle or primary cause of anything. For example, when we say that the having a house to live in was the final cause of this or that house, we merely mean that a man, because he imagined the advantages of a domestic life, desired to build a house. Therefore, having a house to live in, in so far as it is considered as a final cause, is merely this particular desire, which is really an efficient cause, and is considered as primary, because men are usually ignorant of the causes of their desires; for, as I have often said, we are conscious of our actions and desires, but ignorant of the causes by which we are determined to desire anything. . . .

> *"The highest virtue of the mind is to understand or know God."*

The Virtue of Knowing God

The highest good of the mind is the knowledge of God, and the highest virtue of the mind is to know God.

The highest thing which the mind can understand is God, that is to say, Being absolutely infinite, and without whom nothing can be nor can be conceived, and therefore that which is chiefly profitable to the mind, or which is the highest good of the mind, is the knowledge of God. Again, the mind acts only in so far as it understands, and only in so far can it be absolutely said to act in conformity with virtue. To understand, therefore, is the absolute virtue of the mind. But the highest thing which the mind can understand is God (as we have already demonstrated), and therefore the highest virtue of the mind is to understand or know God. Q.E.D. . . .

The good which every one who follows after virtue seeks for himself he will desire for other men; and his desire on their behalf will be greater in proportion as he has a greater knowledge of God.

Men are most profitable to man in so far as they live according to the guidance of reason, and therefore, according to the guidance of reason, we necessarily endeavour to cause men to live according to the guidance of reason. But the good which each person seeks who lives according to the dictates of reason, that is to say, who follows after virtue, is to understand, and therefore the good which each person seeks who follows after virtue he will also desire for other men. Again, desire, in so far as it is related to the mind, is the essence itself of the mind. But the essence of the mind consists in knowledge, which involves the knowledge of God, and without this knowledge the essence of the mind can neither be nor be conceived; and therefore the greater the knowledge of God which the essence of the mind involves, the greater will be the desire with which he who follows after virtue will desire for another the good which he seeks for himself.   Q.E.D.

The good which a man seeks for himself and which he loves he will love more unchangeably if he sees that others love it, and therefore he will endeavour to make others love it; and because this good is common to all and all can rejoice in it, he will endeavour (by the same reasoning) to cause all to rejoice in it, and he will do so the more, the more he rejoices in this good himself. Q.E.D.

> "The good which each person seeks who follows after virtue he will also desire for other men."

He who strives from an affect alone to make others love what he himself loves, and to make others live according to his way of thinking, acts from mere impulse, and is therefore hateful, especially to those who have other tastes and who therefore also desire, and by the same impulse strive to make others live according to their way of thinking.

Again, since the highest good which men seek from an affect is often such that only one person can possess it, it follows that persons who love are not consistent with themselves, and, whilst they delight to recount the praises of the beloved object, fear lest they should be believed. But he who endeavours to lead others by reason does not act from impulse, but with humanity and kindness, and is always consistent with himself.

The Guidance of Reason

Everything which we desire and do, of which we are the cause in so far as we possess an idea of God, or in so far as we know God, I refer to *Religion*. The desire of doing well which is born in us, because we live according to the guidance of reason, I call *Piety*. The desire to join others in friendship to himself, with which a man living according to the guidance of reason is possessed, I call

Chapter 1

Honour. I call that thing *Honourable* which men who live according to the guidance of reason praise; and that thing, on the contrary, I call *Base* which sets itself against the formation of friendship. . . .

It is by the highest right of nature that each person exists, and consequently it is by the highest right of nature that each person does those things which follow from the necessity of his nature; and therefore it is by the highest right of nature that each person judges what is good and what is evil, consults his own advantage as he thinks best, avenges himself, and endeavours to preserve what he loves and to destroy what he hates. If men lived according to the guidance of reason, every one would enjoy this right without injuring any one else. But because men are subject to affects, which far surpass human power or virtue, they are often drawn in different directions, and are contrary to one another, although they need one another's help.

In order, then, that men may be able to live in harmony and be a help to one another, it is necessary for them to cede their natural right, and beget confidence one in the other that they will do nothing by which one can injure the other.

Atheism Motivates People to Behave Ethically

by Friedrich Nietzsche

About the author: Friedrich Nietzsche (1844–1900) was a German philosopher, author, and poet. He is renowned for his statement, "God is dead," by which he meant that religion had lost its meaningfulness and efficacy in modern society. He rejected Christianity, arguing that its values were based on fear and resentment, that it incorrectly accepted all people as equals, and that it denied this world in favor of an illusory other world. Nietzsche's concept of the "superman"—the passionate individual able to control and utilize passions creatively—expressed his view of the ideal manner of human existence. He wrote the books Thus Spake Zarathustra *and* Beyond Good and Evil, *from which this viewpoint is excerpted.*

The human soul and its frontiers, the compass of human inner experience in general attained hitherto, the heights, depths and distances of this experience, the entire history of the soul *hitherto* and its still unexhausted possibilities: this is the predestined hunting-ground for a born psychologist and lover of the "big-game hunt." But how often must he say despairingly to himself: "one man! alas, but one man! and this great forest and jungle!" And thus he wishes he had a few hundred beaters and subtle well-instructed tracker dogs whom he could send into the history of the human soul and there round up *his* game. In vain: he discovers again and again, thoroughly and bitterly, how hard it is to find beaters and dogs for all the things which arouse his curiosity. The drawback in sending scholars out into new and dangerous hunting grounds where courage, prudence, subtlety in every sense are needed is that they cease to be of any use precisely where the "*big* hunt," but also the big danger, begins—precisely there they do lose their keenness of eye and keenness of nose. To divine and establish, for example, what sort of history the problem of *knowledge and conscience* has had in the soul of *homines religiosi* one would oneself perhaps have to be as profound, as wounded, as monstrous as Pascal's intellectual conscience was—and

Excerpted from Friedrich Nietzsche, *Beyond Good and Evil*, translated by R.J. Hollingdale. London: Penguin Classics, 1973. Translation ©1972 by R.J. Hollingdale. Reprinted by permission of Penguin Books Ltd.

then there would still be needed that broad heaven of bright, malicious spirituality capable of looking down on this turmoil of dangerous and painful experiences, surveying and ordering them and forcing them into formulas.—But who could do me this service! And who could have the time to wait for such servants!—They appear too rarely, they are at all times so very improbable! In the end one has to do everything *oneself* if one is to know a few things oneself: that is to say, one has *much* to do!—But a curiosity like mine is after all the most pleasurable of vices—I beg your pardon! I meant to say: the love of truth has its reward in Heaven, and already upon earth.—

Suicide of Reason

The faith such as primitive Christianity demanded and not infrequently obtained in the midst of a sceptical and southerly free-spirited world with a centuries-long struggle between philosophical schools behind it and in it, plus the education in tolerance provided by the *Imperium Romanum*—this faith is *not* that gruff, true-hearted liegeman's faith with which a Martin Luther, say, or an Oliver Cromwell, or some other northern barbarian of the spirit cleaved to his God and his Christianity; it is rather that faith of Pascal which resembles in a terrible fashion a protracted suicide of reason—of a tough, long-lived, worm-like reason which is not to be killed instantaneously with a single blow. The Christian faith is from the beginning sacrifice: sacrifice of all freedom, all pride, all self-confidence of the spirit, at the same time enslavement and self-mockery, self-mutilation. There is cruelty and religious Phoenicianism in this faith exacted of an over-ripe, manifold and much-indulged conscience: its presupposition is that the subjection of the spirit is indescribably *painful*, that the entire past and habitude of such a spirit resists the *absurdissimum* which "faith" appears to it to be. Modern men, with their obtuseness to all Christian nomenclature, no longer sense the gruesome superlative which lay for an antique taste in the paradoxical formula "god on the cross." Never and nowhere has there hitherto been a comparable boldness in inversion, anything so fearsome, questioning and questionable, as this formula: it promised a reevaluation of all antique values.—It is the orient, the *innermost* orient, it is the oriental slave who in this fashion took vengeance on Rome and its noble and frivolous tolerance on Roman "catholicism" of faith; and it has never been faith but always freedom from faith, that half-stoical and smiling unconcern with the seriousness of faith, that has en-

> *"The Christian faith is . . . sacrifice of all freedom, all pride, all self-confidence of the spirit."*

raged slaves in their masters and against their masters. "Enlightenment" enrages: for the slave who wants the unconditional, he understands in the domain of morality too only the tyrannical, he loves as he hates, without nuance, into the depths of him, to the point of pain, to the point of sickness—the great *hid-*

den suffering he feels is enraged at the noble taste which seems to *deny* suffering. Scepticism towards suffering, at bottom no more than a pose of aristocratic morality, was likewise not the least contributory cause of the last great slave revolt which began with the French Revolution.

The Dangers of Christianity

Wherever the religious neurosis has hitherto appeared on earth we find it tied to three dangerous dietary prescriptions: solitude, fasting and sexual abstinence—but without our being able to decide with certainty which is cause here and which effect, or *whether* any relation of cause and effect is involved here at all. The justification of the latter doubt is that one of the most frequent symptoms of the condition, in the case of savage and tame peoples, is the most sudden and most extravagant voluptuousness which is then, just as suddenly, reversed into a convulsion of penitence and a denial of world and will: both perhaps interpretable as masked epilepsy? But nowhere is it more necessary to renounce interpretations: around no other type has there grown up such an abundance of nonsense and superstition, none seems to have hitherto interested men, even philosophers, more—the time has come to cool down a little on this matter, to learn caution: better to look away, *to go away*. . . .

It seems that their Catholicism is much more an intrinsic part of the Latin races than the whole of Christianity in general is of us northerners; and that unbelief consequently signifies something altogether different in Catholic countries from what it does in Protestant—namely a kind of revolt against the spirit of the race, while with us it is rather a return to the spirit (or lack of spirit—) of the race. We northerners are undoubtedly descended from barbarian races also in respect of our talent for religion: we have *little* talent for it. We may except the Celts, who therefore supplied the best soil for the reception of the Christian infection in the north—the Christian ideal came to blossom, so far as the pale northern sun permitted it, in France. How uncongenially pious are to our taste even these latest French sceptics when they have in them any Celtic blood! How Catholic, how un-German does August Comte's sociology smell to us with its Roman logic of the instincts! How Jesuitical that clever and charming cicerone of Port-Royal, Charles-Augustin Sainte-Beuve, despite all his hostility towards the Jesuits! And even more so Ernest Renan: how inaccessible to us notherners is the language of a Renan, in whom every other minute some nothingness of religious tension topples a soul which is in a refined sense voluptuous and relaxed! . . .

What astonishes one about the religiosity of the ancient Greeks is the tremendous amount of gratitude that emanates from it—the kind of man who stands

> *"Why atheism today?—'The father' in God is thoroughly refuted. . . . He does not hear—and if he heard he would still not know how to help."*

thus before nature and before life is a very noble one!—Later, when the rabble came to predominate in Greece, *fear* also overran religion; and Christianity was preparing itself.—

The passion for God: there is the peasant, true-hearted and importunate kind, like Luther's—the whole of Protestantism lacks southern *delicatezza*. There is an oriental ecstatic kind, like that of a slave who has been undeservedly pardoned and elevated, as for example in the case of Augustine, who lacks in an offensive manner all nobility of bearing and desire. There

> **"The concepts 'God' and 'sin' will one day seem to us of no more importance than a child's toy and a child's troubles seem to an old man."**

is the womanly tender and longing kind which presses bashfully and ignorantly for a *unio mystica et physica:* as in the case of Madame de Guyon. In many cases it appears strangely enough as a disguise for the puberty of a girl or a youth; now and then even as the hysteria of an old maid, also as her final ambition—the church has more than once canonized the woman in question.

Hitherto the mightiest men have still bowed down reverently before the saint as the enigma of self-constraint and voluntary final renunciation: why did they bow? They sensed in him—as it were behind the question-mark presented by his fragile and miserable appearance—the superior force that sought to prove itself through such a constraint, the strength of will in which they recognized and knew how to honour their own strength and joy in ruling: they honoured something in themselves when they honoured the saint. In addition to this, the sight of the saint aroused a suspicion in them: such an enormity of denial, of anti-nature, will not have been desired for nothing, they said to themselves. Is there perhaps a reason for it, a very great danger about which the ascetic, thanks to his secret visitors and informants, might possess closer knowledge? Enough, the mighty world learned in face of him a new fear, they sensed a new power, a strange enemy as yet unsubdued—it was the "will to power" which constrained them to halt before the saint. They had to question him—.

In the Jewish "Old Testament," the book of divine justice, there are men, things and speeches of so grand a style that Greek and Indian literature have nothing to set beside it. One stands in reverence and trembling before these remnants of what man once was and has sorrowful thoughts about old Asia and its little jutting-out promontory Europe, which would like to signify as against Asia the "progress of man." To be sure: he who is only a measly tame domestic animal and knows only the needs of a domestic animal (like our cultured people of today, the Christians of "cultured" Christianity included—) has no reason to wonder, let alone to sorrow, among those ruins—the taste for the Old Testament is a touchstone in regard to "great" and "small"—: perhaps he will find the New Testament, the book of mercy, more after his own heart (there is in it a great deal of the genuine delicate, musty odour of devotee and petty soul). To have glued this New Testament, a species of rococo taste in every respect, on to the Old Testament to form a *single* book, as "bible," as "the book of books": that is perhaps the greatest piece of temerity and "sin against the spirit" that literary Europe has on its conscience.

Why Atheism?

Why atheism today?—"The father" in God is thoroughly refuted; likewise "the judge," "the rewarder." Likewise his "free will": he does not hear—and if he heard he would still not know how to help. The worst thing is: he seems incapable of making himself clearly understood: is he himself vague about what he means?—These are what, in course of many conversations, asking and listening, I found to be the causes of the decline of European theism; it seems to me that the religious instinct is indeed in vigorous growth—but that it rejects the theistic answer with profound mistrust. . . .

There is a great ladder of religious cruelty with many rungs; but three of them are the most important. At one time one sacrificed human beings to one's god, perhaps precisely those human beings one loved best—the sacrifice of the first-born present in all prehistoric religions belongs here, as does the sacrifice of the Emperor Tiberius in the Mithras grotto on the isle of Capri, that most horrible of all Roman anachronisms. Then, in the moral epoch of mankind, one sacrificed to one's god the strongest instincts one possessed, one's "nature"; the joy of *this* festival glitters in the cruel glance of the ascetic, the inspired "anti-naturist." Finally: what was left to be sacrificed? Did one not finally have to sacrifice everything comforting, holy, healing, all hope, all faith in a concealed harmony, in a future bliss and justice? Did one not have to sacrifice God himself and out of cruelty against oneself worship stone, stupidity, gravity, fate, nothingness? To sacrifice God for nothingness—this paradoxical mystery of the ultimate act of cruelty was reserved for the generation which is even now arising: we all know something of it already.—

He who, prompted by some enigmatic desire, has, like me, long endeavoured to think pessimism through to the bottom and to redeem it from the half-Christian, half-German simplicity and narrowness with which it finally presented itself to this century, namely in the form of the Schopenhaueran philosophy; he who has really gazed with an Asiatic and more than Asiatic eye down into the most world-denying of all possible modes of thought—beyond good and evil and no longer, like Buddha and Arthur Schopenhauer, under the spell and illusion of morality—perhaps by that very act, and without really intending to, may have had his eyes opened to the opposite ideal: to the ideal of the most exuberant, most living and most world-affirming man, who has not only learned to get on and treat with all that was and is but who wants to have it again *as it was and is* to all

"What wisdom there is in the fact that men are superficial."

eternity, insatiably calling out *da capo* not only to himself, but to the whole piece and play, and not only to a play but fundamentally to him who needs precisely this play—and who makes it necessary: because he needs himself again and again—and makes himself necessary—What? And would this not be—
circulus vitiosus deus?

> *"Piety ... [is] the subtlest and ultimate product of the fear of truth."*

With the strength of his spiritual sight and insight the distance, and as it were the space, around man continually expands: his world grows deeper, ever new stars, ever new images and enigmas come into view. Perhaps everything on which the spirit's eye has exercised its profundity and acuteness has been really but an opportunity for its exercise, a game, something for children and the childish. Perhaps the most solemn concepts which have occasioned the most strife and suffering, the concepts "God" and "sin," will one day seem to us of no more importance than a child's toy and a child's troubles seem to an old man—and perhaps "old man" will then have need of another toy and other troubles—still enough of a child, an eternal child!

Indifference to Religion

Has it been observed to what extent a genuine religious life (both for its favourite labour of microscopic self-examination and that gentle composure which calls itself "prayer" and which is a constant readiness for the "coming of God"—) requires external leisure or semi-leisure, I mean leisure with a good conscience, inherited, by blood, which is not altogether unfamiliar with the aristocratic idea that work *degrades*—that is to say, makes soul and body common? And that consequently modern, noisy, time-consuming, proud and stupidly proud industriousness educates and prepares precisely for "unbelief" more than anything else does? Among those in Germany for example who nowadays live without religion, I find people whose "free-thinking" is of differing kinds and origins but above all a majority for those in whom industriousness from generation to generation has extinguished the religious instincts: so that they no longer have any idea what religions are supposed to be for and as it were merely register their existence in the world with a kind of dumb amazement. They feel they are already fully occupied, these worthy people, whether with their businesses or with their pleasures, not to speak of the "fatherland" and the newspapers and "family duties": it seems that they have no time at all left for religion, especially as it is not clear to them whether it involves another business or another pleasure—for they tell themselves it is not possible that one goes to church simply to make oneself miserable. They are not opposed to religious usages; if participation in such usages is demanded in certain cases, by the state for instance, they do what is demanded of them as one does so many things—with patient and modest seriousness and without much curiosity and discomfort—it is only that they live too much aside and outside even to feel the need for any for or against in such things. The great majority of German middle-class Protestants can today be numbered among these indifferent people, especially in the great industrious centres of trade and commerce; likewise the great majority of industrious scholars and the entire university equipage (excepting the theologians, whose possibility and presence there provides the psychologist with ever more and ever subtler enigmas to solve). Pious or even merely church-going people seldom realize *how much* good will, one might even say willfulness, it requires nowadays for a German scholar to take the problem of religion seriously; his whole trade (and as said above, the tradesmanlike industriousness to which his modern conscience obliges him) disposes him to a superior, almost good-natured merriment in regard to religion, sometimes mixed with a mild contempt directed at the "uncleanliness" of spirit which he presupposes wherever one still belongs to the church. It is only with the aid of history (thus *not* from his personal experience) that the scholar succeeds in summoning up a reverent seriousness and a certain shy respect towards religion; but if he intensifies his feelings towards it even to the point of feeling grateful to it, he has still in his own person not got so much as a single step closer to that which still exists as church or piety: perhaps the reverse. The practical indifference to religious things in which he was born and raised is as a rule sublimated in him into a caution and cleanliness which avoids contact with religious people and things; and it can be precisely

> **"Christianity has been the most fatal kind of self-presumption ever."**

the depth of his tolerance and humanity that bids him evade the subtle distress which tolerance itself brings with it.—Every age has its own divine kind of naïvety for the invention of which other ages may envy it—and how much naïvety, venerable, childlike and boundlessly stupid naïvety there is in the scholar's belief in his superiority, in the good conscience of his tolerance, in the simple unsuspecting certainty with which his instinct treats the religious man as an inferior and lower type which he himself has grown beyond and *above*—he, the little presumptuous dwarf and man of the mob, the brisk and busy head- and handyman of "ideas," of "modern ideas"!

Fear Leads People to Religion

He who has seen deeply into the world knows what wisdom there is in the fact that men are superficial. It is their instinct for preservation which teaches them to be fickle, light and false. Here and there, among philosophers as well as artists, one finds a passionate and exaggerated worship of "pure forms": let no one doubt that he who *needs* the cult of surfaces to that extent has at some time or other made a calamitous attempt to get *beneath* them. Perhaps there might even exist an order of rank in regard to these burnt children, these born artists who can find pleasure in life only in the intention of falsifying its image (as it were in a long-drawn-out revenge on life—): one could determine the degree to which life has been spoiled for them by the extent to which they want to see its image falsified, attenuated and made otherworldly and divine—one could include the *homines religiosi* among the artists as their *highest* rank. It is the profound suspicious fear of an incurable pessimism which compels whole millennia to cling with their teeth to a religious interpretation of existence: the fear born of that instinct which senses that one might get hold of the truth *too soon*, before mankind was sufficiently strong, sufficiently hard,

> *"A shrunken, almost ludicrous species, a herd animal, something full of good will, sickly and mediocre has been bred, the European of today."*

sufficient of an artist. . . . Piety, the "life in God," would, viewed in this light, appear as the subtlest and ultimate product of the *fear* of truth, as the artist's worship of an intoxication before the most consistent of all falsifications, as the will to inversion of truth, to untruth at any price. Perhaps there has up till now been no finer way of making man himself more beautiful than piety: through piety man can become to so great a degree art, surface, play of colours, goodness, that one no longer suffers at the sight of him.—

To love men *for the sake of God*—that has been the noblest and most remote feeling attained to among men up till now. That love of man without some sanctifying ulterior objective is one piece of stupidity and animality *more*, that the inclination to this love of man has first to receive its measure, its refinement, its grain of salt and drop of amber from a higher inclination—whatever man it was who first felt and "experienced" this, however much his tongue may have faltered as it sought to express such a delicate thought, let him be holy and venerated to us for all time as the man who has soared the highest and gone the most beautifully astray! . . .

The Danger of Saving the Weak

Among men, as among every other species, there is a surplus of failures, of the sick, the degenerate, the fragile, of those who are bound to suffer. . . . Now what is the attitude of [Christianity and Buddhism] towards this *surplus* of unsuccessful cases? They seek to preserve, to retain in life, whatever can in any way be preserved, indeed they side with it as a matter of principle as religions *for sufferers*, they maintain that all those who suffer from life as from an illness are in the right, and would like every other feeling of life to be counted false and become impossible. However highly one may rate this kindly preservative solicitude, inasmuch as, together with all the other types of man, it has been and is applied to the highest type, which has hitherto almost always been the type that has suffered most: in the total accounting the hitherto *sovereign* religions are among the main reasons the type "man" has been kept on a lower level—they have preserved too much of that *which ought to perish*. We have inestimable benefits to thank them for; and who is sufficiently rich in gratitude not to be impoverished in face of all that the "spiritual men" of Christianity, for example, have hitherto done for Europe! And yet, when they gave comfort to the suffering, courage to the oppressed and despairing, a staff and stay to the irresolute, and lured those who were inwardly shattered and had become savage away from society into monasteries and houses of correction for the soul: what did they have to do in addition so as thus, with a good conscience, as a matter of principle, to work at the preservation of everything sick and suffering, which means in fact and truth at the *corruption of the European race?* Stand all evaluations *on their head—that* is what they had to do! And smash the strong, contaminate great hopes, cast suspicion on joy in beauty, break down everything autocratic, manly, conquering, tyrannical, all the instincts proper to the highest and most successful of the type "man," into uncertainty, remorse of conscience, self-destruction, indeed reverse the whole love of the earthly and of dominion over the earth into hatred of the earth and the earthly—*that* is the task the church set itself and had to set itself, until in its evaluation "unworldliness," "unsensuality," and "higherman" were finally fused together into *one* feeling. Supposing one were able to view the strangely painful and at the same time coarse and subtle comedy of European Christianity with the mocking and unconcerned eye of an Epicurean god, I believe there would be no end to one's laughter and amazement: for does it not seem that *one* will has dominated Europe for eighteen centuries, the will to make of man a *sublime abortion?* But he who, with an opposite desire, no longer Epicurean but with some divine hammer in his hand, approached this almost deliberate degeneration and stunting of man such as constitutes the European Christian (Pascal for instance), would he not have to cry out in rage, in pity, in horror: "O you fools, you presumptuous, pitying fools, what have you done! Was this a work for your hands! How you have bungled and botched my beautiful stone! What a thing for *you* to take upon yourselves!"—What I am saying is: Christianity has been the most fatal kind of self-presumption ever. Men not high or hard enough for the artistic refashioning of *mankind*; men not strong or farsighted enough for the sublime self-constraint needed to *allow* the foreground law of thousandfold failure and perishing to prevail; men not noble enough to see the abysmal disparity in order of rank and abysm of rank between man and man—it is *such* men who, with their "equal before God," have hitherto ruled over the destiny of Europe, until at last a shrunken, almost ludicrous species, a herd animal, something full of good will, sickly and mediocre has been bred, the European of today.

Biological Imperative Causes People to Act Ethically

by Edward O. Wilson

About the author: *Scientist and author Edward O. Wilson is the Pellegrino University Research Professor at Harvard University, as well as Honorary Curator in Entomology for Harvard's Museum of Comparative Zoology. His books include* The Diversity of Life, On Human Nature, *and* Consilience: The Unity of Knowledge, *from which the following viewpoint is adapted.*

Centuries of debate on the origin of ethics come down to this: Either ethical principles, such as justice and human rights, are independent of human experience, or they are human inventions. The distinction is more than an exercise for academic philosophers. The choice between these two understandings makes all the difference in the way we view ourselves as a species. It measures the authority of religion, and it determines the conduct of moral reasoning.

Competing Assumptions

The two assumptions in competition are like islands in a sea of chaos, as different as life and death, matter and the void. One cannot learn which is correct by pure logic; the answer will eventually be reached through an accumulation of objective evidence. Moral reasoning, I believe, is at every level intrinsically consilient with—compatible with, intertwined with—the natural sciences. (I use a form of the word "consilience"—literally a "jumping together" of knowledge as a result of the linking of facts and fact-based theory across disciplines to create a common groundwork of explanation—because its rarity has preserved its precision.)

Every thoughtful person has an opinion on which premise is correct. But the split is not, as popularly supposed, between religious believers and secularists. It is between transcendentalists, who think that moral guidelines exist outside the human mind, and empiricists, who think them contrivances of the mind. In simplest terms, the options are as follows: *I believe in the independence of moral values, whether from God or not,* and *I believe that moral values come from human beings alone, whether or not God exists.*

Theologians and philosophers have almost always focused on transcendentalism as the means to validate ethics. They seek the grail of natural law, which comprises freestanding principles of moral conduct immune to doubt and compromise. Christian theologians, following Saint Thomas Aquinas's reasoning in *Summa Theologiae,* by and large consider natural

> *"If we explore the biological roots of moral behavior, . . . we should be able to fashion a wise and enduring ethical consensus."*

law to be an expression of God's will. In this view, human beings have an obligation to discover the law by diligent reasoning and to weave it into the routine of their daily lives. Secular philosophers of a transcendental bent may seem to be radically different from theologians, but they are actually quite similar, at least in moral reasoning. They tend to view natural law as a set of principles so powerful, whatever their origin, as to be self-evident to any rational person. In short, transcendental views are fundamentally the same whether God is invoked or not. . . .

The Empiricist View of Ethics

In the empiricist view, ethics is conduct favored consistently enough throughout a society to be expressed as a code of principles. It reaches its precise form in each culture according to historical circumstance. The codes, whether adjudged good or evil by outsiders, play an important role in determining which cultures flourish and which decline.

The crux of the empiricist view is its emphasis on objective knowledge. Because the success of an ethical code depends on how wisely it interprets moral sentiments, those who frame one should know how the brain works, and how the mind develops. The success of ethics also depends on how accurately a society can predict the consequences of particular actions as opposed to others, especially in cases of moral ambiguity.

The empiricist argument holds that if we explore the biological roots of moral behavior, and explain their material origins and biases, we should be able to fashion a wise and enduring ethical consensus. The current expansion of scientific inquiry into the deeper processes of human thought makes this venture feasible. . . .

I am an empiricist. On religion I lean toward deism, but consider its proof largely a problem in astrophysics. The existence of a God who created the universe (as envisioned by deism) is possible, and the question may eventually be settled, perhaps by forms of material evidence not yet imagined. Or the matter may be forever beyond human reach. In contrast, and of far greater importance to humanity, the idea of a biological God, one who directs organic evolution and intervenes in human affairs (as envisioned by theism), is increasingly contravened by biology and the brain sciences.

The same evidence, I believe, favors a purely material origin of ethics, and it meets the criterion of consilience: causal explanations of brain activity and evolution, while imperfect, already cover most facts known about behavior we term "moral.". . .

The argument of the empiricist has roots that go back to Aristotle's *Nicomachean Ethics* and, in the beginning of the modern era, to David Hume's *A Treatise of Human Nature* (1739–1740). The first clear evolutionary elaboration of it was by Charles Darwin, in *The Descent of Man* (1871). . . .

[In the empiricist view,] the individual is seen as predisposed biologically to make certain choices. Through cultural evolution some of the choices are hardened into precepts, then into laws, and, if the predisposition or coercion is strong enough, into a belief in the command of God or the natural order of the universe. The general empiricist principle takes this form: *Strong innate feeling and historical experience cause certain actions to be preferred; we have experienced them, and have weighed their consequences, and agree to conform with codes that express them. Let us take an oath upon the codes, invest our personal honor in them, and suffer punishment for their violation.* The empiricist view concedes that moral codes are devised to conform to some drives of human nature and to suppress others. *Ought* is the translation not of human nature but of the public will, which can be made increasingly wise and stable through an understanding of the needs and pitfalls of human nature. The empiricist view recognizes that the strength of commitment can wane as a result of new knowledge and experience, with the result that certain rules may be desacralized, old laws rescinded, and formerly prohibited behavior set free. It also recognizes that for the same reason new moral codes may need to be devised, with the potential of being made sacred in time.

> *"Causal explanations of brain activity and evolution . . . cover most facts known about behavior we term 'moral.'"*

The Origin of Moral Instincts

If the empiricist world view is correct, *ought* is just shorthand for one kind of factual statement, a word that denotes what society first chose (or was coerced) to do, and then codified. The naturalistic fallacy is thereby reduced to the naturalistic problem. The solution of the problem is not difficult: *ought* is the product of a material process. The solution points the way to an objective grasp of the origin of ethics.

A few investigators are now embarked on just such a foundational inquiry. Most agree that ethical codes have arisen by evolution through the interplay of biology and culture. . . .

What have been thought of as moral sentiments are now taken to mean moral instincts (as defined by the modern behavioral sciences), subject to judgment according to their consequences. Such sentiments are thus derived from epigenetic rules—hereditary biases in mental development, usually conditioned by emotion, that influence concepts and decisions made from them. The primary origin of moral instincts is the dynamic relation between cooperation and defection. The essential ingredient for the molding of the instincts during genetic evolution in any species is intelligence high enough to judge and manipulate the tension generated by the dynamism. That level of intelligence allows the building of complex mental scenarios well into the future. It occurs, so far as is known, only in human beings and perhaps their closest relatives among the higher apes.

A way of envisioning the hypothetical earliest stages of moral evolution is provided by game theory, particularly the solutions to the famous Prisoner's Dilemma. Consider the following typical scenario of the dilemma. Two gang members have been arrested for murder and are being questioned separately. The evidence against them is strong but not irrefutable. The first gang member believes that if he turns state's witness, he will be granted immunity and his partner will be sentenced to life in prison. But he is also aware that his partner has the same option, and that if both of them exercise it, neither will be granted immunity. That is the dilemma. Will the two gang members independently defect, so that both take the hard fall? They will not, because they agreed in advance to remain silent if caught. By doing so, both hope to be convicted on a lesser charge or escape punishment altogether. Criminal gangs have turned this principle of calculation into an ethical precept: Never rat on another member; always be a stand-up guy. Honor does exist among thieves. The gang is a society of sorts; its code is the same as that of a captive soldier in wartime, obliged to give only name, rank, and serial number.

The Benefits of Cooperation

In one form or another, comparable dilemmas that are solvable by cooperation occur constantly and everywhere in daily life. The payoff is variously money, status, power, sex, access, comfort, or health. Most of these proximate rewards are converted into the universal bottom line of Darwinian genetic fitness: greater longevity and a secure, growing family.

> "Moral codes are devised to conform to some drives of human nature and to suppress others."

And so it has most likely always been. Imagine a Paleolithic band of five hunters. One considers breaking away from the others to look for an antelope on his own. If successful, he will gain a large quantity of meat and hide—five times as much as if he stays with the band and they are successful. But he knows from experience that his chances of success are very low, much less than the chances of the band of five working together. In addition, whether successful alone or not, he will suffer animosity from the others for lessening their prospects. By custom the band members remain together and share equitably the animals they kill. So the hunter stays. He also observes good manners in doing so, especially if he is the one who makes the kill. Boastful pride is condemned, because it rips the delicate web of reciprocity.

> *"Ethical codes have arisen by evolution through the interplay of biology and culture."*

Now suppose that human propensities to cooperate or defect are heritable: some people are innately more cooperative, others less so. In this respect moral aptitude would simply be like almost all other mental traits studied to date. Among traits with documented heritability, those closest to moral aptitude are empathy with the distress of others and certain processes of attachment between infants and their caregivers. To the heritability of moral aptitude add the abundant evidence of history that cooperative individuals generally survive longer and leave more offspring. Following that reasoning, in the course of evolutionary history genes predisposing people toward cooperative behavior would have come to predominate in the human population as a whole.

Such a process repeated through thousands of generations inevitably gave rise to moral sentiments. With the exception of psychopaths (if any truly exist), every person vividly experiences these instincts variously as conscience, self-respect, remorse, empathy, shame, humility, and moral outrage. They bias cultural evolution toward the conventions that express the universal moral codes of honor, patriotism, altruism, justice, compassion, mercy, and redemption.

The dark side of the inborn propensity to moral behavior is xenophobia. Because personal familiarity and common interest are vital in social transactions, moral sentiments evolved to be selective. People give trust to strangers with effort, and true compassion is a commodity in chronically short supply. Tribes cooperate only through carefully defined treaties and other conventions. They are quick to imagine themselves the victims of conspiracies by competing groups, and they are prone to dehumanize and murder their rivals during periods of severe conflict. They cement their own group loyalties by means of sacred symbols and ceremonies. Their mythologies are filled with epic victories over menacing enemies.

The complementary instincts of morality and tribalism are easily manipulated. Civilization has made them more so. Beginning about 10,000 years ago, a tick in geological time, when the agricultural revolution started in the Middle East, in China, and in Mesoamerica, populations increased tenfold in density over those of hunter-gatherer societies. Families settled on small plots of land, villages proliferated, and labor was finely divided as a growing minority of the populace specialized as craftsmen, traders, and soldiers. The rising agricultural societies became increasingly hierarchical. As chiefdoms and then states thrived on agricultural surpluses, hereditary rulers and priestly castes took power. The old ethical codes were transformed into coercive regulations, always to the advantage of the ruling classes. About this time the idea of law-giving gods originated. Their commands lent the ethical codes overpowering authority—once again, no surprise, in the interests of the rulers.

The Complexity of Human Nature

Because of the technical difficulty of analyzing such phenomena in an objective manner, and because people resist biological explanations of their higher cortical functions in the first place, very little progress has been made in the biological exploration of the moral sentiments. Even so, it is astonishing that the study of ethics has advanced so little since the nineteenth century. The most distinguishing and vital qualities of the human species remain a blank space on the scientific map. I doubt that discussions of ethics should rest upon the freestanding assumptions of contemporary philosophers who have evidently never given thought to the evolutionary origin and material functioning of the human brain. In no other domain of the humanities is a union with the natural sciences more urgently needed.

> *"What have been thought of as moral sentiments are now taken to mean moral instincts."*

When the ethical dimension of human nature is at last fully opened to such exploration, the innate epigenetic rules of moral reasoning will probably not prove to be aggregated into simple instincts such as bonding, cooperativeness, and altruism. Instead the rules will most probably turn out to be an ensemble of many algorithms, whose interlocking activities guide the mind across a landscape of nuanced moods and choices.

Such a prestructured mental world may at first seem too complicated to have been created by autonomous genetic evolution alone. But all the evidence of biology suggests that just this process was enough to spawn the millions of species of life surrounding us. Each kind of animal is furthermore guided through its life cycle by unique and often elaborate sets of instinctual algorithms, many of which are beginning to yield to genetic and neurobiological analyses. With all these examples before us, we may reasonably conclude that human behavior originated the same way. . . .

The Origins of Religion

The same reasoning that aligns ethical philosophy with science can also inform the study of religion. Religions are analogous to organisms. They have a life cycle. They are born, they grow, they compete, they reproduce, and, in the fullness of time, most die. In each of these phases religions reflect the human organisms that nourish them. They express a primary rule of human existence:

Whatever is necessary to sustain life is also ultimately biological.

Successful religions typically begin as cults, which then increase in power and inclusiveness until they achieve tolerance outside the circle of believers. At the core of each religion is a creation myth, which explains how the world began and how the chosen people—those subscribing to the belief system—arrived at its center. Often a mystery, a set of secret instructions and formulas, is available to members who have worked their way to a higher state of enlightenment. The medieval Jewish cabala, the trigradal system of Freemasonry, and the carvings on Australian aboriginal spirit sticks are examples of such arcana. Power radiates from the center, gathering converts and binding followers to the group. Sacred places are designated, where the gods can be importuned, rites observed, and miracles witnessed.

The devotees of the religion compete as a tribe with those of other religions. They harshly resist the dismissal of their beliefs by rivals. They venerate self-sacrifice in defense of the religion.

The tribalistic roots of religion are similar to those of moral reasoning and may be identical. Religious rites, such as burial ceremonies, are very old. It appears that in the late Paleolithic period in Europe and the Middle East bodies were sometimes placed in shallow graves, accompanied by ocher or blossoms; one can easily imagine such ceremonies performed to invoke spirits and gods. But, as theoretical deduction and the evidence suggest, the primitive elements of moral behavior are far older than Paleolithic ritual. Religion arose on a foundation of ethics, and it has probably always been used in one manner or another to justify moral codes.

Religion and Instincts

The formidable influence of the religious drive is based on far more, however, than just the validation of morals. A great subterranean river of the mind, it gathers strength from a broad spread of tributary emotions. Foremost among them is the survival instinct. "Fear," as the Roman poet Lucretius said, "was the first thing on earth to make the gods." Our conscious minds hunger for a permanent existence. If we cannot have everlasting life of the body, then absorption into some immortal whole will serve. *Anything* will serve, as long as it gives the individual meaning and somehow stretches into eternity that swift passage of the mind and spirit lamented by Saint Augustine as the short day of time.

> *"Cooperative individuals generally survive longer and leave more offspring."*

The understanding and control of life is another source of religious power. Doctrine draws on the same creative springs as science and the arts, its aim being the extraction of order from the mysteries and tumult of the material world. To explain the meaning of life it spins mythic narratives of the tribal history, populating the cosmos with protective spirits and gods. The existence of the supernatural, if accepted, testifies to the existence of that other world so desperately desired.

Religion is also mightily empowered by its principal ally, tribalism. The shamans and priests implore us, in somber cadence, *Trust in the sacred rituals, become part of the immortal force, you are one of us. As your life unfolds, each step has mystic significance that we who love you will mark*

> **"The dark side of the inborn propensity to moral behavior is xenophobia."**

with a solemn rite of passage, the last to be performed when you enter that second world, free of pain and fear.

If the religious mythos did not exist in a culture, it would quickly be invented, and in fact it has been invented everywhere, thousands of times through history. Such inevitability is the mark of instinctual behavior in any species, which is guided toward certain states by emotion-driven rules of mental development. To call religion instinctive is not to suppose that any particular part of its mythos is untrue—only that its sources run deeper than ordinary habit and are in fact hereditary, urged into existence through biases in mental development that are encoded in the genes.

Biological Imperative Does Not Cause People to Act Ethically

by Philip Yancey

About the author: *Philip Yancey is a columnist for* Christianity Today *and a frequent contributor to* Books & Culture *and other magazines. He is also the author of numerous books, including* What's So Amazing About Grace? *and* The Jesus I Never Knew.

A representative of Generation X named Sam told me he had been discovering the strategic advantages of truth. As an experiment, he decided to stop lying. "It helps people picture you and relate to you more reliably," he said. "Truth can be positively beneficial in many ways."

I asked what would happen if he found himself in a situation where it would prove *more* beneficial for him to lie. He said he would have to judge the context, but he was trying to prefer not-lying.

An Unprecedented Dilemma

For Sam, the decision to lie or tell the truth involved not morality but a social construct, to be adopted or rejected as a matter of expedience. In essence, the source of moral authority for Sam is himself, and that in a nutshell is the dilemma confronting moral philosophy in the postmodern world.

Something unprecedented in human history is brewing: a rejection of external moral sources altogether. Individuals and societies have always been im-moral to varying degrees. Individuals (never an entire society) have sometimes declared themselves amoral, professing agnosticism about ethical matters. Only recently, however, have serious thinkers entertained the notion of un-morality: that there is no such thing as morality. A trend prefigured by Friedrich Nietzsche, prophesied by Fyodor Dostoyevsky, and analyzed presciently by C.S. Lewis in *The Abolition of Man* is now coming to fruition. The very concept of

Excerpted from "Nietzsche Was Right," by Philip Yancey, *Books & Culture*, January/February 1998. Reprinted with permission from the author.

morality is undergoing a profound change, led in part by the advance guard of a new science called "evolutionary psychology."

So far, however, the pioneers of unmorality have practiced a blatant contradiction. Following in the style of Jean-Paul Sartre, who declared that meaningful communication is impossible even as he devoted his life to communicating meaningfully, the new moralists first proclaim that morality is capricious, perhaps even a joke, then

> *"If we learn our morality from nature, . . . why should not the strong exercise their 'natural rights' over the weak?"*

proceed to use moral categories to condemn their opponents. These new high priests lecture us solemnly about multiculturalism, gender equality, homophobia, and environmental degradation, all the while ignoring the fact that they have systematically destroyed any basis for judging such behavior right or wrong. The emperor so quick to discourse about fashion happens to be stark naked.

For example, George Williams wrote a landmark book in 1966 entitled *Adaptation and Natural Selection,* which portrayed all behavior as a genetically programmed expression of self-interest. Yet later, after examining some of the grosser examples of animal behavior, he concluded that "Mother Nature is a wicked old witch. . . . Natural selection really is as bad as it seems and . . . it should be neither run from nor emulated, but rather combatted."

Williams neglected to explain what allowed him, a product of pure natural selection, to levitate above nature and judge it morally bankrupt. He may understandably disapprove of animal cannibalism and rape, but on what grounds can he judge them "evil"? And how can we—or why should we—combat something programmed into our genes?

Lest I sound like a cranky middle-aged moralist, I should clarify at the beginning that to me the real question is not why modern secularists oppose traditional morality; it is on what grounds they defend *any* morality.

The Morality of the Church

We hold these truths to be probable enough for pragmatists, that all things looking like men were evolved somehow, being endowed by heredity and environment with no equal rights but very unequal wrongs. . . Men will more and more realize that there is no meaning in democracy if there is no meaning in anything. And there is no meaning in anything if the universe has not a center of significance and an authority that is the author of our rights.

—G.K. Chesterton

In a great irony, the "politically correct" movement defending the rights of women, minorities, and the environment often positions itself as an enemy of the Christian church when, in historical fact, the church has contributed the very underpinnings that make such a movement possible. Christianity brought an end to slavery, and its crusading fervor also fueled the early labor movement, women's suffrage, human-rights campaigns, and civil rights. According to Robert Bellah, "there has not been a major issue in the history of the United States on which religious bodies did not speak out, publicly and vociferously."

It was no accident that Christians pioneered in the antislavery movement, for their beliefs had a theological impetus. Both slavery and the oppression of women were based, anachronistically, on an embryonic form of Darwinism. Aristotle had observed that

> Tame animals are naturally better than wild animals, yet for all tame animals there is an advantage in being under human control, as this secures their survival. And as regards the relationship between male and female, the former is naturally superior, the latter inferior, the former rules and the latter is subject. By analogy, the same must necessarily apply to mankind as a whole. Therefore all men who differ from one another by as much as the soul differs from the body or man from a wild beast (and that is the state of those who work by using their bodies, and for whom that is the best they can do)—these people are slaves by nature, and it is better for them to be subject to this kind of control, as it is better for the other creatures I have mentioned. . . . It is clear that there are certain people who are free and certain people who are slaves by nature, and it is both to their advantage, and just, for them to be slaves. . . . From the hour of their birth, some men are marked out for subjection, others for rule.

Cross out the name *Aristotle* and read the paragraph again as the discovery of a leading evolutionary psychologist. No one is proposing the reimposition of slavery, of course—but why not? If we learn our morality from nature, and if our only rights are those we create for ourselves, why should not the strong exercise their "natural rights" over the weak?

"Scientists who dismantle any notion of good and evil nevertheless must fall back on those categories of judgment."

As Alasdair MacIntyre remarks in *After Virtue,* modern protesters have not abandoned moral argument, though they have abandoned any coherent platform from which to make a moral argument. They keep using moral terminology—it is *wrong* to own slaves, rape a woman, abuse a child, despoil the environment, discriminate against homosexuals—but they have no "higher authority" to which to appeal to make their moral judgments. MacIntyre concludes,

> Hence the *utterance* of protest is characteristically addressed to those who already *share* the protestors' premises. The effects of incommensurability ensure that protestors rarely have anyone else to talk to but themselves. This is not to say that protest cannot be effective; it is to say that it cannot be *rationally* effective and that its dominant modes of expression give evidence of a certain perhaps unconscious awareness of this.

In the United States, we prefer to settle major issues on utilitarian or pragmatic grounds. But philosophers including Aristotle and David Hume argued powerfully in favor of slavery on those very grounds. Adolf Hitler pursued his genocidal policies against the Jews and "defective" persons on utilitarian grounds. Unless modern thinkers can locate a source of moral authority somewhere else than in the collective sentiments of human beings, we will always be vulnerable to dangerous swings of moral consensus.

What Makes a Person Good?

A man who has no assured and ever-present belief in the existence of a personal God or of a future existence with retribution or reward, can have for his rule of life, as far as I can see, only to follow those impulses and instincts which are the strongest or which seem to him the best ones.

—Charles Darwin

Christina Hoff Sommers tells of a Massachusetts educator attempting to teach values-clarification to her class of sixth-graders. One day her canny students announced that they valued cheating and wanted the freedom to practice it in class. Hoist with her own petard, the teacher could only respond that since it was *her* class, she insisted on honesty; they would have to exercise their dishonesty in other places. In view of such an approach to morality, should it surprise us to learn from surveys that half of all students cheat? What restrains the other half?

What makes a person good? What is "good" anyway? Moral philosophers such as Charles Taylor and Alasdair MacIntyre argue convincingly that many people in the modern world can no longer answer that question coherently.

A friend of mine named Susan, a committed Christian, told me that her husband did not measure up and she was actively looking for other men to meet her needs for intimacy. When Susan mentioned that she rose early each day to "spend an hour with the Father," I asked, "In your meetings with the Father, do any moral issues come up that might influence this pending decision about leaving your husband?"

Susan bristled: "That sounds like the response of a white Anglo-Saxon male. The Father and I are into relationship, not morality. Relationship means being wholly supportive and standing alongside me, not judging." I gently pointed out that we all make judgments in our relationships. Had not she judged her husband incapable of meeting her needs? Susan fended off my arguments, and we moved on to more congenial topics.

> *"Psychopaths represent the group that acts most consistently to the new code of 'unmorality.'"*

Like many moderns, my friend Susan has moved the locus of morality from an external to an internal source, a change that traces back to the Romantic movement and its new celebration of the individual. In his essay "Self-Reliance," Ralph Waldo Emerson proclaimed that everyone should "Trust thyself," for divinity resides in every person. What if your intuitions are evil? Emerson did not back down: "They do not seem to me to be such; but if I am the devil's child, I will live then from the devil. No law can be sacred to me but that of my nature."

Jean-Jacques Rousseau, a grandfather of Romanticism, had followed the dictates of his heart by abandoning five infants born to his illiterate servant-mistress. Of course, one could find many such scandalous incidents before the outbreak of Romanticism. The real change was more subtle and subterranean. From Aristotle onward, the West had always perceived "the good" as an external code, neither mine nor yours. Though one could choose to break the code, it remained an external code above and beyond the reach of any individual. With Romanticism, the code moved inside so as to become radically subjective. The individual self began writing his or her own moral script.

> *"Without a belief in God or afterlife, a person can only follow those impulses and instincts that are the strongest."*

The Genetic Explanation

Nearly two centuries after the flowering of Romanticism, we are witnessing the consequences of that unmooring of the moral code. In a strange twist, whereas Augustine viewed evil as a perversion of good, modern ethicists view goodness as a manifestation of selfishness. Everything we do, including every act of nobility or altruism, serves a hidden purpose: to enhance oneself or to perpetuate genetic material. Challenged to explain Mother Teresa's behavior, sociobiologist Edward O. Wilson pointed out that she was secure in the service of Christ and in her belief in immortality; in other words, believing she would get her reward, she acted on that "selfish" basis.

Robertson McQuilkin, a college president who resigned in order to care for his Alzheimer's-afflicted wife, attended a seminar in which a researcher reported that, in her study of 47 couples facing terminal illness, she had predicted with 100 percent accuracy who would die soonest, simply by observing the relationship between husband and wife. "Love helps survival," she concluded. From there, McQuilkin went directly to another session in which an expert listed reasons why families might choose to keep an ailing family member at home rather than in a nursing facility. Noting that the reasons all boiled down to economic necessity or guilt feelings, McQuilkin asked, "What about love?" "Oh," replied the expert, "I put that under guilt."

While redefining goodness, modern society has simultaneously discarded the notion of sin. In the movie *Ironweed,* Helen, an alcoholic, informs God at a candlelit altar, "You may call them sins; I call them decisions." Increasingly, bad actions are seen as neither sins nor decisions, rather as the outworking of behavior patterns hardwired into our brains. A murderer goes free on the grounds that eating Twinkies contributed to his mental instability; a national authority excuses political consultant Dick Morris's adultery as the normal biological response to an environment of power and status.

I have already mentioned that scientists who dismantle any notion of good and evil nevertheless must fall back on those categories of judgment. This kind of moral schizophrenia expresses itself at every level of society. We must cling to some form of morality or both person and society will swirl apart. Yet individuals find themselves unable to articulate a code of morality, and even less able to keep any code. Abbie Hoffman, a radical leader in the 1960s, complained, "I've never liked guilt-tripping. I've always left the concept of sin to the Catholic Church. When I was four, my mother said, 'There's millions of people starving in China. Eat your dinner.' I said, 'Ma, name one.'" Yet this rebel against guilt trips ran a distinctively "moral" campaign against a repressive society and an unjust war.

Pathology

After interviewing average Americans to determine why they behave the way they do, Robert Bellah and his associates came up with a primary ethic of "self-fulfillment." Bellah acknowledges that most people want to be "good" even though few can articulate a reason for it. In their roles as parents, spouses, and citizens, ordinary people demonstrate qualities of sacrifice, fidelity, and altruism. They act, in Bellah's opinion, out of "habits of the heart" rooted primarily in America's Christian heritage. Remove those habits of the heart, and the true pathology of modern times comes to light.

> *"Civilization holds together when a society learns to place moral values above the human appetites for power, wealth, violence, and pleasure."*

Indeed, psychopaths represent the group that acts most consistently to the new code of "unmorality." Immune to social pressures, these deviants live out the courage of their nonconvictions.

"Character," says Robert Coles, "is how you behave when no one is looking." Coles goes on to suggest that for the conscientious, those with a highly developed moral sense, "someone is always 'looking,' even if we are as solitary as Thoreau at Walden." But for the psychopath or sociopath, the "unmoral" person, no one is ever looking. The unmoral person believes in no outside source of moral authority and inside hears only the "terrible silences of an emotionally abandoned early life or the demonic voices of a tormented childhood."

Prison interviews with two mass murderers, Jeffrey Dahmer and Ted Bundy, bear out Coles's observation. Both were asked how they could possibly do the things they did. Both replied that, at the time, they did not believe in God and felt accountable to no one. They started with petty cruelty, then moved to torture of animals and people, and then murder. Nothing internal or external stopped them from making the descent to unmorality—they felt no twinge of guilt. Ironically, both mass murderers followed to logical conclusion the principle laid down by Charles Darwin a century ago—that without a belief in God or after-life, a person can only follow those impulses and instincts that are the strongest.

We read daily in the newspapers the tragic results of those who follow their strongest impulses. Bill Moyers asked the late Joseph Campbell what results when a society no longer embraces a religion or powerful mythology. "What we've got on our hands," Campbell replied; ". . . read the *New York Times*."

Not only for psychopaths, but for everyday sinners, the practice of looking inside for moral guidance is fraught with danger. Woody Allen, a sophisticated, brilliant filmmaker, granted an interview to *Time* magazine in order to counter his wife's accusations against sexual abuse of her children and to explain his affair with his 21-year-old adopted Korean daughter. "The heart wants what it wants," said Allen. "There's no logic to those things. You meet someone and you fall in love and that's that."

Symptoms of Moral Illness

It is easy to see that the moral sense has been bred out of certain sections of the population, like the wings have been bred off certain chickens to produce more white meat on them. This is a generation of wingless chickens.

—Flannery O'Connor

What happens when an entire society becomes populated with wingless chickens? I need not dwell on the contemporary symptoms of moral illness in the United States: our rate of violent crime has quintupled in my lifetime; a third of all babies are now born out of wedlock; half of all marriages end in divorce; the richest nation on earth has a homeless population larger than the entire population of some nations. These familiar symptoms are just that, symptoms. A diagnosis would look beyond them to our loss of a teleological sense. "Can one be a saint if God does not exist? That is the only concrete problem I know of today," wrote Albert Camus in *The Fall*.

Civilization holds together when a society learns to place moral values above the human appetites for power, wealth, violence, and pleasure. Historically, it has always relied on religion to provide a source for that moral authority. In fact, according to Will and Ariel Durant, "There is no significant example in history, before our time, of a society successfully maintaining moral life without the aid of religion." They added the foreboding remark, "The greatest question of our time is not communism versus individualism, not Europe versus America, not even the East versus the West; it is whether men can live without God."

> *"There is no significant example in history, before our time, of a society successfully maintaining moral life without the aid of religion."*

Vàclav Havel, a survivor of a civilization that tried to live without God, sees the crisis clearly:

I believe that with the loss of God, man has lost a kind of absolute and universal system of coordinates, to which he could always relate everything, chiefly himself. His world and his personality gradually began to break up into separate, incoherent fragments corresponding to different, relative, coordinates.

On moral issues—social justice, sexuality, marriage and family, definitions of life and death—society badly needs a moral tether, or "system of coordinates" in Havel's phrase. Otherwise, our laws and politics will begin to reflect the same kind of moral schizophrenia already seen in individuals. . . .

Redefining Morality

Critics of Christianity correctly point out that the church has proved an unreliable carrier of moral values. The church has indeed made mistakes, launching Crusades, censuring scientists, burning witches, trading in slaves, supporting tyrannical regimes. Yet the church also has an inbuilt potential for self-correction because it rests on a platform of transcendent moral authority. When human beings take upon themselves the Luciferian chore of redefining morality, untethered to any transcendent source, all hell breaks loose.

In Nazi Germany, and also in the Soviet Union, China, and Cambodia, the government severed morality from its roots. Nazi propagandists dismissed biblical revelation as "Jewish swindle" and emphasized instead the general revelation they observed in the natural order of creation. Vladimir Lenin ordered Russians to adopt "the Revolutionary Conscience" as opposed to their natural conscience.

> *"The church . . . rests on a platform of transcendent moral authority."*

Our century is the first in which societies have attempted to form their moral codes without reference to religion. We have had the chance to "take the world in our own hands," in Camus's phrase. Modern humanity, Camus said, "launches the essential undertaking of rebellion, which is that of replacing the reign of grace by the reign of justice." The results are in: perhaps 100 million deaths under Hitler, Joseph Stalin, Mao Tse-tung, and Pol Pot attributable to this grand new reign of justice.

Today, of course, apart from China, the threat posed by communism has disappeared. We in the West rest secure, even triumphant. Yet the bats are out of the cage. The spiritual sources that fed both Nazism and communism are still with us.

We look back with horror on the Nazi campaign to exterminate the mentally defective. But not long ago the newsletter of a California chapter of Mensa, the organization for people with high IQs, published an article proposing the elimination of undesirable citizens, including the retarded and the homeless. Modern China requires the abortion of defective fetuses, including those diagnosed with retardation, and kills "unauthorized" babies born to one-child families. And in some states in the United States, due largely to pressures from insurance companies, the incidence of Down syndrome children has dropped 60 percent; the rest are aborted before birth.

Religion Is the Basis of Morality

In his study *Morality: Religious and Secular,* Basil Mitchell argues that, since the eighteenth century, secular thinkers have attempted to make reason, not religion, the basis of morality. None has successfully found a way to establish an *absolute* value for the individual human person. Mitchell suggests that secular thinkers can establish a relative value for people, by comparing people to animals, say, or to each other; but the idea that every person has an absolute value came out of Christianity and Judaism before it and is absent from every other ancient philosophy or religion.

The Founding Fathers of the United States, apparently aware of the danger, made a valiant attempt to connect individual rights to a transcendent source. Overruling Thomas Jefferson, who had made only a vague reference to "the Laws of Nature and of Nature's God," they insisted instead on including the words "unalienable" and "endowed by their Creator." They did so in order to secure such rights in a transcendent Higher Power, so that no human power could attempt to take them away. Human dignity and worth derive from God's.

Chapter 2

Is American Business Becoming More Ethical?

Business Ethics: An Overview

by Lisa Genasci

About the author: *Lisa Genasci is a reporter for the Associated Press news service.*

Bath Iron Works Corp. was in a quandary. A major customer had asked the boat builder to participate in an under-the-boards investigation of one of its suppliers. Although the customer was key to Bath's survival, purchasing manager Patrick Thomas wasn't sure how to handle the request. So he went to the company's ethics officer, who in turn took the problem to the chief executive.

Within 12 hours the Maine company had established its position: It would not participate in the investigation unless the supplier was notified about what was going on. Eventually, the customer accepted Bath's stand.

The Beginnings of a Change?

Business ethics may sound like an oxymoron, with seemingly endless news reports about bad behavior at a spectrum of companies. . . .

Wall Street in the 1980s was rife with insider trading. The defense industry has seen some of the most egregious examples of impropriety, with companies such as United Technologies Corp. and Loral Corp. pleading guilty to charges from Pentagon procurement scandals.

But partly in response to hefty fines and other government action—and also because it makes business sense—some companies are introducing ethics into their corporate culture in a big way.

They are rethinking or formalizing codes of conduct, establishing hot lines for employees to call for guidance on nebulous issues and training employees in personal responsibility.

"We're in a once-in-200-years change," said Gerald Ross, a top management consultant and author with Michael Kay of the book *Toppling the Pyramids, Redefining the Way Companies Are Run.*

In 1991, Nynex Corp. opened an office of ethics and business conduct, intro-

Excerpted from "The Case for Ethics," by Lisa Genasci, *The Washington Times,* April 23, 1995. Reprinted with permission from the Associated Press.

duced training seminars and set up guidelines for employees, customers and vendors. The company estimates 75 percent of management employees have gone through ethics training. In 1994, the ethics office received 3,000 calls.

Texas Instruments Inc. has had a written code of ethics for 35 years, but in the mid-1980s the company set up a more formal program, complete with an ethics office, in-house news reports, training sessions and a hot line.

"Ethics is part of our business strategy. It doesn't just come from the need to comply," said Carl Skooglund, the company's ethics director.

A Growing Trend

The Ethics Resource Center in Washington late in 1994 published the results of a national survey that showed a growing percentage of companies have formal ethics programs.

According to the survey, 60 percent have codes of ethics, 33 percent have training in business conduct, and 33 percent have an ethics office where employees can receive advice or report questionable activities.

Observers point to several reasons for the trend.

Many companies are looking to ethics to help guide them through the increasingly complex and competitive business climate as they become more international and restructure their operations.

"Values that on the surface seem soft can be powerful," Mr. Ross said. "As we move through the 1990s and hierarchies are flattened, we have to rely on values to keep companies together. It's the new glue."

The trend toward global business and the growing diversity of work forces have challenged ideas about how a company should operate.

"Previously, one could assume that everyone knew everyone else and understood the code," said James Kuhn, a management professor at Columbia Business School. "Today you can't assume a common background."

Furthermore, employers are able to quantify the savings a good ethics program can bring.

In late 1991, the U.S. Sentencing Commission set new federal sentencing guidelines. Now, if companies can show they have cooperated with investigations into an in-house problem and can show strong ethics and compliance programs, federal judges must take those efforts into account when issuing sentences for corporate wrongdoing.

"Some companies are introducing ethics into their corporate culture in a big way."

Legal standards generally are tougher these days, with enforcement stricter in many areas, including the environment and workplace-related concerns.

"Corporations are beginning to realize ethics initiatives can help reduce risk and limit liability," said W. Michael Hoffman, executive director of the Ethics Officers' Association, which is affiliated with the Center for Business Ethics at

Bentley College in Waltham, Mass.

But he said companies also are beginning to recognize that a strong ethics program can be good for business in other ways including attracting and retaining the best work force. "Employees feel good about working for a company that is trying to do the right thing," Mr. Hoffman said.

The sense that a company is behaving ethically can also translate into improved productivity and better product quality, he said.

In many cases, ethical behavior has become an imperative. A better-informed public may resist investing in or buying products from companies with damaged reputations, said Harvard business professor Lynn Sharp Paine.

Many company owners and executives prefer doing business with a firm that has a good reputation.

Scandals Continue to Erupt

Still, there is the sense that far from becoming more ethical, companies' values are loosening as yet another scandal hits the press.

Ethical conduct is harder to maintain in corporations today than it was 20 years ago, said Gary Edwards, president of the Ethics Resource Center.

"The way corporations are organized and managed creates environments that make decent people come to believe top management expects them to do whatever they must to survive," Mr. Edwards said.

Part of the problem, he and others said, is that the corporate restructurings of recent years have made people wary of losing their jobs. They see people who don't meet corporate goals being shoved out the door, while those who meet them, sometimes at any cost, are promoted.

"Companies are making unrealistic commitments, driving goals and objectives through the corporation," said Mr. Edwards, whose nonprofit group advises companies on the practical application of business ethics.

His group's survey showed that nearly a third of workers felt pressured by their companies to violate corporate policy in order to achieve business objectives.

In addition, the elimination of layers of management in recent years has meant that remaining employees are often left to their own resources with less oversight, Mr. Edwards said.

"Companies are shaking out the system because it just isn't sustainable," Mr. Ross said. "But once you take the police system away, what holds the corporation together?"

Meanwhile, the stakes are much higher, with millions or billions of dollars shifted at the touch of a computer key.

"If there are common values, the company can trust people and move forward," Mr. Kuhn said.

Still, in the Ethics Resource Center study, nearly a third of employees said they had witnessed conduct in the past year that they felt violated corporate policy or the law. But fewer than half of them said they had reported the action.

Many Businesses Are Presenting a Facade of Social Responsibility

by Betsy Reed

About the author: *Betsy Reed is the coeditor of* Real World International *and a former coeditor of* Dollars and Sense, *a bimonthly magazine concerning economic issues.*

Late in the fall of 1997, some 600 business leaders—including CEOs, marketing directors, and investors in some of the nation's largest corporations—gathered at the Sheraton Grande, a giant nonunion conference center in downtown L.A., for the fifth annual meeting of an organization called Business for Social Responsibility. BSR started out as a small network of profit-minded liberals in the Ben-and-Jerry's mold, eager to prove that you can save the planet, help the poor, and make money at the same time. But in the last few years the organization has welcomed hundreds of mainstream companies into its ranks, such as Dayton Hudson (owner of the Target stores), Phillips-Van Heusen, The Gap, Levi Strauss, Mitsubishi, Wal-Mart, Monsanto, Reebok, and Nike.

Ethics as a Marketing Strategy

At the conference, even the more straitlaced business types could not get enough of the feel-good stuff. Participants were especially keen on the concepts of cause-related marketing (attaching a brand name to a charity to sell products) and strategic philanthropy (making charitable contributions with corporate interests in mind). Session after jam-packed session examined innovative means of making good works pay off. At one, a bright young marketer from Timberland explained the financial logic of offering free boots to City Year youth activists (i.e., so their hip, urban friends would want some, too); at another, a company called SAS Industries presented diagrams in a slide show demonstrating how on-site child care and medical care minimizes the amount of time employees spend away from their desks.

Reprinted from "The Business of Social Responsibility," by Betsy Reed, *Dollars and Sense,* May/June 1998. Reprinted with permission from *Dollars and Sense.* Article available at www.dollarsandsense.org/issues/may98/reed.html.

No one seemed to notice the dissonance generated by the pooling of such helpful hints. If this conference had a mantra, it was that being socially responsible is, by definition, good for business; what will benefit society will benefit the company, and vice versa. Old-school corporate executives, stockholders, and radical economists alike might be skeptical of such a premise, but at a lunch table or break-out session at this event, expressing any doubt in its inherent validity felt like assailing the tooth fairy in front of a classroom of second-graders.

In a panel discussion focusing on human rights abroad, a patient professor stood for ten minutes rephrasing his query for representatives of Liz Claiborne, Patagonia, and Nike: "What do you do when treating workers well impairs your ability to compete? Isn't there sometimes a trade-off between being socially responsible and maximizing profit?" In reply, Nike's director of labor practices, named Dusty Kidd, claimed that such questions were obsolete now that companies have figured out that a contented workforce is more productive. The woman representing Liz Claiborne called the issue of a living wage a "media-driven distraction" from all of the voluntary steps the apparel industry has taken toward greater social responsibility. For their part, audience members emphasized the positive influence of consumer social consciousness on corporate behavior, and conversely, the deterrent effect of the high public relations costs on corporate misbehavior.

> *"Companies are placing [growing value] on cultivating an appearance of social responsibility, whatever their actual practices."*

Sometimes the discrepancy between a firm's self-image and reality was almost surreal. Later on at the same session, Nike's Kidd presented a video of a factory in Vietnam. The camera followed a Vietnamese inspector on his rounds, interviewing plucky, smiling workers, running his hands over gleaming production equipment, and visiting immaculate homes. Unfortunately for Nike, two days later—while the conference was still going on—a story appeared on the front page of the *New York Times* about conditions in Vietnamese Nike plants, where workers were being exposed to carcinogens at 177 times safe levels, and were being paid just $10 for a 65-hour workweek (far longer than local law allows).

What rapidly was becoming apparent, from all the videos and glossy brochures and slide shows and speeches, was the very real—and growing—value that companies are placing on cultivating an appearance of social responsibility, whatever their actual practices. In part this is a consequence of rising interest among investors in the stocks of so-called socially responsible companies. Socially screened investments—very broadly defined—grew 85% from 1996 to 1997, from $639 billion to $1.185 trillion, according to a recent study by Social Investment Forum. Frequently, social screens merely eliminate firms with extreme public image problems, such as tobacco companies. The Domini 400 Social Index, one of the leading purveyors of social research for concerned investors, is lenient enough to include half of the S&P 500, and until late in October 1997 Nike was among them (it was deleted due to "international labor controversies").

Perhaps even more significant, though, is the value of brand-image for firms marketing consumer goods to a broad segment of the public. A Roper-Cone poll found that 78% of Americans weigh a company's social reputation when making buying decisions. Cutting-edge marketing strategy prescribes building relationships with consumers by conveying an impression of what the whole company stands for, which is supposed to breed long-lasting brand loyalty.

Cultivating an Image

A look at the contrasting cases of Reebok and Nike shows just how important clever public relations, combined with targeted philanthropy, can be for a company.

Over the years, Reebok has made many friends in the international human rights community and, by extension, everywhere else. The late-80s "Human Rights Now!" concert tour, featuring Sting and Bruce Springsteen, garnered huge publicity in Central Europe and several Third World countries, associating the brand with compelling pop icons. And the Reebok Human Rights Awards recognizes and rewards genuinely inspiring activists. In 1998, winners included Rana Husseini, a Jordanian journalist who exposed widespread "honor crimes" against women (including murder) that go virtually unpunished; and Dydier Kamundo of Congo, one of the few activists to challenge the military's systematic torture of prisoners.

Nike, meanwhile, has largely neglected the realm of strategic philanthropy. Its clumsy efforts to appear friendly to women through its "If you let me play" ad campaign have backfired, with the National Organization for Women and other women's groups mounting a campaign to publicize the exploitation of women and girls in Nike plants in Vietnam, China, and Indonesia.

Nike has been the target of boycotts, repeated media investigations, and international protest. Reebok has experienced almost none of these things. To be sure, Nike's overall labor record is worse, but not that much worse. There's still plenty to complain about with Reebok: The company's contracting factories in Southern China are riddled with wage, hour, and health violations, and Reebok continues to exploit child labor to stitch soccer balls in Pakistan despite a public pledge to put an end to the practice.

> *"The rhetoric of corporate social responsibility can be an effective disguise for seriously antisocial behavior."*

The danger is that the rhetoric of corporate social responsibility can be an effective disguise for seriously antisocial behavior. But there is, of course, another side to that coin: namely the opportunity to point out hypocrisy at its most egregious.

American Workers Are Becoming Less Ethical

by *Society*

About the author: Society *is a bimonthly periodical that focuses on issues concerning social science.*

Nearly half, 48 percent, of U.S. workers admit to unethical or illegal acts during 1996. Those include one or more from a list of 25 actions, including cheating on an expense account, discriminating against coworkers, paying or accepting kickbacks, secretly forging signatures, trading sex for sales and looking the other way when environmental laws are violated.

The survey of 1,324 randomly selected workers, managers, and executives in multiple industries was sponsored by the Ethics Officer Association and the American Society of Chartered Life Underwriters & Chartered Financial Consultants. The 236-page report is especially sobering because workers were asked only to list violations that they attributed to "pressure" due to such things as long hours, sales quotas, job insecurity, balancing work and family, and personal debt. It didn't ask about unethical or illegal action for other reasons such as greed, revenge, and blind ambition. The survey's margin of error is plus or minus 3 percentage points.

Also sobering is that workers say it's getting worse. Fifty-seven percent say they feel more pressure to be unethical than five years ago and 40 percent say it's gotten worse over the last year.

Lapses Vary

Many workers might consider some of the 25 ethical violations far less serious, such as calling in sick when they're feeling well. But that's really theft of time, and the problem is "just phenomenal," says Cindy Franklin, president of Background Bureau, a company in the booming business of checking the backgrounds of job applicants.

Constant ethical violations have made workers so callous that deception passes for good salesmanship, Franklin says. "If someone can talk me into buying an $8,000 copier rather than one that sells for $4,200, they're going to get a pat on the back. I see that as unethical if all I need is the $4,200 model."

But unethical and illegal action by employees is taking a heavy toll. Most employee theft goes unreported, but employee-screening company Guardsmark estimates it at $120 billion a year. Retail stores lose more to employee theft than to shoplifting, according to a University of Florida survey. Entry-level restaurant and fast food employees confidentially admit to stealing an average $239 a year in cash and merchandise, according to a separate survey by McGraw-Hill/London House.

Another survey of 2,500 cases of employee fraud by the Association of Certified Fraud Examiners says small businesses suffered a median loss of $120,000 per occurrence. A survey by CCH shows that the more sick leave companies give employees, the more days they call in sick. The federal government successfully sues for more than $100 million a year, mostly from defense contractors and doctors and hospitals that overbill. That's four times the rate it recovered 10 years ago, says Peter Chatfield, a partner at the law firm Phillips & Cohen, which has eight full-time lawyers working on fraudulent billing against the government.

Although the survey blames ethics violations on pressure, workers in marketing/advertising reported themselves to be under the least pressure to be unethical, yet committed more unethical acts than any other industry except that of computers and software.

Pressure and Stress Contribute

Most ethics experts agree that job pressure is the leading cause of unethical behavior by workers. And if anyone doubts pressure exists: 2.4 percent of all workers and 3.2 percent of senior executives have considered suicide over the past year due to pressure, the survey found. Among senior executives who happened to fill out the questionnaire during a time of high stress, 5.4 percent said they were contemplating suicide.

Workers in manufacturing and health care reported the most pressure to act unethically or illegally. But they do not act on it nearly as often as computer/software workers.

Those high-tech employees say they are more than twice as likely as the average worker to put inappropriate pressure on others, withhold important information, discriminate against coworkers, engage in copyright/software infringement, forge someone's name, and misuse or steal company property.

> *"Constant ethical violations have made workers so callous that deception passes for good salesmanship."*

The survey was taken during good economic times. Pressure, and resulting ethics violations, would likely turn worse in an economic slump.

Yet there are nuggets of hope in the ethics survey. In a "startling shift in public opinion," only 15 percent of U.S. workers surveyed believe poor ethics is an inevitable byproduct of business, says Ed Petry, executive director of the Ethics Officer Association. "In the late 1970s and 1980s, business ethics was an oxymoron, a contradiction in terms."

> *"Unethical and illegal action by employees is taking a heavy toll."*

The need to meet said budget or profit goals ranked sixth among 23 factors that workers said could trigger them to act unethically or illegally. Other top factors include balancing work and family, poor leadership, work hours and work load, and little recognition for achievements.

Other survey findings:

• Most workers feel some pressure to act unethically or illegally on the job (56 percent), but far fewer (17 percent) feel a high level of pressure to do so. Forty-eight percent say they actually made at least one unethical or illegal action in the past year.

• Mid-level managers most often reported a high level of pressure to act unethically or illegally (20 percent). Employees at large companies cited such pressure more than those at small businesses (21 percent vs. 14 percent).

• High levels of pressure were reported more often by those with a high school diploma or less (21 percent) vs. college graduates (13 percent).

• Men (74 percent) and women (78 percent) say they feel their families have been neglected to some extent because of workplace pressure. Women (34 percent) more than men (24 percent) say balancing work and family causes significant pressure.

• Workers say the best ways to curb ethical violations are better communication and more open dialogue (73 percent), and serious commitment by management to address the issue (71 percent).

• The most common ethical (16.1 percent) violation is cutting corners on quality control. Nearly 1 in 10 say they lied to customers and 1 in 20 lied to superiors. One out of every 40 workers say that, due to pressure, they had an affair with a business associate or contact.

Business Students Are Increasingly Unethical

by Marianne M. Jennings

About the author: *Marianne M. Jennings is a professor of legal and ethical studies in the business college at Arizona State University. She is also the director of the university's Lincoln Center for Applied Ethics.*

One day in the mid-1980s, the dean of the business school where I teach called me in and declared that we should begin teaching ethics courses. Why? I asked. We had been sending students to the philosophy department for that.

"We're losing majors," the dean explained. "They come back from their ethics course believing capitalism is a tool of the devil, and they're changing their major to liberal arts." So we began a course in ethics, designed to guide business students through the importance of honesty and fairness in a capitalist system.

Alas, my M.B.A. students arrive already trained in fashionable academic socialism. "Capitalism is the source of all poverty," wrote one student. And another: "Most people in business are in it for money." Well, I hope so—but he meant it disparagingly. After reading Michael Novak's book *Business as a Calling,* one student remarked: "It's a stretch to say that capitalism and democracy go together and have religious origins." Another averred that "there's too much of a gap between the rich and poor for his premise to be true."

It's always a challenge to teach business to Marxists and it strikes me that an M.B.A. may not be their best career path. But business schools themselves are partly to blame for their students' antibusiness attitudes. You'd think business schools would be immune to political correctness, but no such luck. Accreditation standards for the American Assembly of Collegiate Schools of Business have begun to read like a cross between an affirmative action plan and a Peace Corps mission statement. Goals for recruiting faculty and students mention demographic diversity, but not merit. Indeed, the standard on business-school faculty specifies only that a school must have "sufficient academic and professional qualifications . . . *in aggregate* [emphasis mine]." Not all your professors have to be qualified.

Curriculum standards dictate that the course of study emphasize "ethical and global issues; the influence of political, social, legal and regulatory, environmental and technological issues, and the impact of demographic diversity on organizations." Likewise, current literature on business-school reform and curriculum content, when not beating the drums for diversity, urges such ed-school fads as "cooperative learning," "team teaching" and "portfolio grading." And the hottest research in business theory stresses such trendy ideas as "stakeholders," "critical thinking" and "empowerment," at the expense of the nuts and bolts of accounting, economics, mathematics and statistics.

All this makes it very hard to teach business ethics. Students feel as if they have already sold their souls by entering an M.B.A. program, so they are resigned to, and comfortable with, all manner of ethical mischief. In short, they condone unethical conduct not because they're Gordon Gekko-style supercapitalists, but because they're guilty liberals.

One student asked me: "If it meant that you could get the operation your mother can't afford but needs to survive, would you embezzle $1 million?"

No, I said.

"Why, you heartless wench," he replied. "No wonder I'm getting a 'C' in this class."

Today's college students, trained as moral relativists, are perplexed at best by universal rules. Among Americans in the 18–34 age group, 79% believe that there are no absolute standards in ethics, according to a survey conducted in 1997 by the Lutheran Brotherhood, an insurance company. A recent poll of M.B.A. students conducted by a pair of business professors found that 73% would hire a competitor's employee to obtain trade secrets. The same survey found that only 60% of *convicted criminals* would do so. One student's response when asked if he would leave a note if he hit a parked car in a parking lot was, "No, because I don't have much money."

Plato, Aristotle, Peter Drucker and Milton Friedman have little impact on my students, who resent being subjected to the "white male perspective on ethics." They equate ethics with correct views on social and political issues rather than with honesty and integrity. One guest speaker in my class, an executive for a media concern, drew some criticism for his po-

> *"Students feel as if they have already sold their souls by entering an M.B.A. program, so they are . . . comfortable with all manner of ethical mischief."*

sition that he always fires employees who do not act with integrity. One student dismissed him because "he accepted cigarette ads." Likewise, many of my students are deeply offended by high levels of executive pay, deplore stock options and believe that a company's gay-rights position is a litmus test for morality.

They were but children during the Reagan years, but they recite the Gordon Gekko creed of "Greed is good" with great familiarity, and they believe business spawned the homeless.

They take it for granted that businesses cheat and are oddly resigned to it. Cooking the books is not a moral leap for them. Mention the dishonesty in the earnings-management techniques of Cendant or Bausch & Lomb and the likely response is: "Everyone does it," or, "That's what M.B.A.s are trained to do," or, "That keeps a company going—it's hard to know when you've crossed the line."

> *"They take it for granted that businesses cheat and are oddly resigned to it."*

Oh well, if I can't teach ethics, I can teach fear. The danger of getting caught is a good motivator. If these students enter the business world with trepidation, it will be thanks to this heartless wench. They will have learned that the law still catches and disciplines businesses and executives who don't play by the rules.

Executives Are Greedy

by Ellen Goodman

About the author: *Ellen Goodman is the associate editor of the* Boston Globe *and a nationally syndicated columnist.*

It's not that I envy the corporate titans. It's just that I have a small failure of imagination.

Every time I try to envision myself as Disney CEO Michael Eisner, I get stuck at the same place. There I am in front of the mirror saying to myself, "Let's see, I earned $575 million last year. Yeah, that seems about right. I'm worth that."

I'm pleased that he doesn't suffer from low self-esteem, but how does he get his mind around those numbers? For that matter, go figure the worth of Sanford I. Weill, the head of Citigroup that runs those nifty ads on the Golf Channel saying, "How Money Works Now." This is how money works now for Weill: He got paid $166 million in 1998.

Then of course, there's GE's John F. Welch Jr. His executive compensation—the word compensation sounds as if he's been working in the coal mines—rang in at $83 million.

How do they measure their value? Ho hum, another day, another quarter-million dollars?

Capitalist Greed

What brings on this particular rant are the annual *Wall Street Journal* and *Business Week* reports on executive pay. We are again invited to gawk at the most garish CEO blossoms on the nation's money tree.

There was a time when J.P. Morgan was considered an icon of pure capitalist greed. But J.P. had a rule that the operating CEOs of his companies couldn't earn more than 20 times what the hired hands earned. By 1980, the average CEO was earning 42 times what the average worker was earning.

Guess what it is now? In 1998, the CEOs at major companies earned 419 times the pay of the average blue-collar worker. And to make it more obvious, the CEO pay at 350 companies ballooned 36 percent in 1998. Workers got a 2.7 percent raise.

Of course these men—and they are almost exclusively white men—don't get this in a weekly paycheck. Most of it comes in stock options. Nor do they compare their worth—mirror, mirror, on the wall—to the average worker. They compare their compensation to the other boys in the CEO club.

But now there is just the itsy-bitsiest notion that maybe, in the words of the *Wall Street Journal* headline, "Enough is Enough." Maybe CEOs shouldn't be getting megabucks if workers are getting pink slips. Maybe the value of the company isn't entirely due to the guy on top.

It isn't just journalists with mirrors and weak imaginations who are suggesting this. Shareholders in a group called Responsible Wealth are trying a new tactic. These members—including the great-great-granddaughter of a Standard Oil founder and the great-grandson of Oscar Mayer—have filed resolutions to get corporations to agree that there should be some defined ratio between CEO and worker pay.

They haven't set a number. They aren't saying that we should go back to J.P. Morgan. But as Scott Klinger, the director of the Responsible Wealth program at United for a Fair Economy, says: "We want to get a discussion going on whether the value of a company has been created by a single person or all employees. We want shareholders to discuss whether it makes sense to focus the cost cutting knife on the floor while executive pay goes up."

> *"There should be some defined ratio between CEO and worker pay."*

In looking over proxy statements, it became apparent that the only criteria for CEO pay was other CEO pay. As Klinger says, "Each statement said they were paying above average." It was like Lake Wobegon where all the children were above average. This thinking kept pushing up CEO pay.

But in April 1999, a vote will come up for some cap on the CEO-worker ratio at the annual meeting of Citigroup. That's where Sanford Weill "earned" his $166 million while his company began laying off some 10,000 workers.

A day later, it will be General Electric. GE's $83 million John Welch was on *Business Week*'s list of CEOs who gave shareholders the least for their money. There will be eight companies facing votes in the spring of 1999.

There are others taking on the issue of CEO pay. Unions, whose pension funds make them heavy investors, are also going for a new look in the financial mirror.

Right now, the May 1999 issue of *Money* magazine has a cover line boasting, "Everyone's Getting Rich!" But everyone isn't getting rich. In the growing gap, the top 1 percent of households now have more wealth than the bottom 95 percent.

The folks at Responsible Wealth are saying that shareholders are also stakeholders in society. The cap they are trying on for size is a thinking cap.

Businesses Are Increasingly Promoting Ethical Behavior

by John Davidson

About the author: *John Davidson is a writer based in Austin, Texas.*

For those of us who experienced the moral climate of the corporate world in the '80s, it's a shock to discover that ethics has become an industry—a billion-dollar growth industry. Ten years ago, ethics programs in companies were rare; the business world was exultantly Darwinian, a dog-eat-dog, corporation-devour-corporation kind of place. The marketplace was by definition amoral, but we celebrated it nonetheless.

Today, 45 percent of companies with 500 or more employees have ethics programs. The Ethics Officer Association, founded in 1991, has more than 400 members, many employed by Fortune 500 companies, and there are 75 to 100 centers for business ethics scattered around the country. Not only are corporations concerned with internal conduct, they're also sponsoring ethics training in public schools. In the ultimate case of privatization, some companies contend that they are taking over the role of government in teaching values and citizenship.

The relationship between today's ethics boom and the moral squalor of the "greed is good" '80s is not coincidental. It began in 1986, when the Reagan administration appointed a congressional commission to investigate the scandal-plagued defense industry. The commission threatened the industry with federal policing if it didn't clean up its act. Leading defense companies responded by joining together to pass the Defense Industry Initiative (DII), which included a recommendation that companies establish ethics training. In 1991, when Congress revised the Federal Sentencing Guidelines for Organizations to include provisions that would make penalties harsher and more consistent for white-collar crimes, the DII recommendations were written into the revisions. According to the guidelines, penalties could be mitigated for corporations that had ethics programs; the fines for miscreant companies without them could be as much as four times higher.

Winning Employees Over

The bottom-line implications of failing to encourage ethical behavior are all too obvious—Texaco's loss in a race-discrimination suit with a $154 million judgment against the company, the Archer Daniels Midland Co.'s $100 million fine for price fixing, Mercury Finance's $2.2 billion drop in stock values due to overstating profits. But ethics can also be the glue that holds a corporation together, says Carol Marshall, vice president of ethics and business conduct at Lockheed Martin Corp. "In 1995, the Lockheed Martin merger brought together 16 corporate cultures," Marshall explains. "We needed a process that would unite these diverse cultures, and talking about values and principles was a way to do it. After the merger, the board of directors adopted six core values as our code of conduct. We want people to bring their personal values to work and not park them at the door."

Lockheed Martin initiated what Marshall refers to as "top-down cascade training." The chairman of the board trains the staffers who report directly to him. They in turn train their staff. Eventually, all 200,000 employees hear the same core message delivered at annual training sessions. Lockheed Martin also created The Ethics Challenge, a board game based on the "Dilbert" comic strip in which players must deal with ethical dilemmas, and set up a toll-free helpline for employees. "When we started the helpline in 1995, one-third of the calls were anonymous," says Marshall, "but the number has been decreasing and is down by 25 percent. This is an important statistic. It means that people trust the process. They are no longer willing to subvert their personal values to the bottom line."

Diversity in the workplace has played a prominent role in the ethics industry. "We're now living in a multicultural world, and we can't assume that everyone thinks the same way," says Michael Daigneault, president of the Ethics Resource Center in Washington, D.C. "The influx of women, for example, fostered a genuine dialogue about ethics and gender issues. Because of women, we've had to stop and think about the relationship between individuals and what we expect of each other."

"Not only are corporations concerned with internal conduct, they're also sponsoring ethics training in public schools."

But for many companies, these internal programs come too late. "Companies no longer know who they've got working for them," says Michael Josephson, founder of the Josephson Institute of Ethics in Marina del Rey, California. "In one survey, 25 to 40 percent of high school students say they would lie on a résumé; 39 percent say they've stolen something in the last year; two-thirds say they've cheated on an exam." How does this show up in the workplace? "Twenty percent of the workers in one survey said they had lied to their employer about something important in the last year," Josephson says. "Sixty percent said they had a low level of confidence in the integrity of their corporation's internal reports, and 33 percent believed there was a 'kill the messenger syndrome' that forced them to lie and cover up. Corporations have made tremendous investments in literacy because they need workers who can read. Now they're investing in moral literacy because they also need an honest work force."

Taking the Message Public

For that reason, companies are moving more forcefully into the community. "Through their programs, corporations are taking on a new leadership role in society," says Daigneault. "They are an important influence in people's lives. They're positively reinforcing people, saying that it's okay to talk about values and ethical principles. People used to look to the government to teach values. Companies have begun to take over that role.

"Take the public schools," Daigneault continues. "There was a time when most people believed the school system's job was to educate children and to create good citizens. Then, in the 1950s and '60s, schools adopted a philosophy of 'values clarification.' Instead of telling students what to think, teachers would lead them through the process of examining values. When the big problems were gum chewing and talking in class, values clarification worked fine. These days, the big problems are rape, weapons, and drugs, and values clarification isn't as useful."

The current antidote is "character education," which teaches the basic values—honesty, respect for others—that society expects of its members. Bell Atlantic Corp., in conjunction with the Ethics Resource Center, has developed a curriculum package for character education that it is making available to school administrators nationwide. Jacquelyn B. Gates, Bell Atlantic's ethics VP, says the company got interested in public education because employees were calling its ethics hotline with concerns about their children's schools. "If people perceive that corporations have the responsibility to intervene," says Daigneault, "it's because corporations have the power."

With major corporations pushing values, one has to wonder what the larger effect on society might be. Are we headed toward, if not the Age of Aquarius, a more moral climate?

"There are hopeful signs," says Michael Josephson, "but you can't point to any social change. Ethics might be just another issue du jour, like total quality management, risk taking, and thinking outside the box. Phases and fads go through the corporate world. We trained 2,000 IRS employees, yet the IRS has no institutional memory that we were ever there. It's too early to tell what the impact of all this activity will be, but it would be a mistake to dismiss the movement."

Ethical Practices Benefit Corporations

by Stephen Butler

About the author: *Stephen Butler is the chief executive officer of KPMG Peat Marwick, a financial services firm.*

Because of the very nature of what KPMG [Peat Marwick] does and its stature as one of the Big Six [accounting firms], we have access to and knowledge of the best practices of many world-class companies. That inside look has taught me many things, not the least of which is: good ethics means good business. One way you as business leaders can protect your position is to install, enforce and re-enforce a culture and standard of ethical conduct within your organization that can't be challenged.

Ethics and Self-Interest

Now some of you may be thinking it's unusual for me to stand up here and promote higher ethical standards in corporate America, especially since I am a CEO that is strongly focused on the bottom line! Or you may be thinking that I'm doing this to infer that KPMG wears the white hats and our competitors, black ones. . . . Not so. Neither of these reasons are valid or are driving my comments today.

And I'm not a tree hugger either. I do want to be able to look myself in the mirror each morning and respect the person I see. I want to know that my 13-year-old son, John, can and does admire me, and that my mother does too.

But I want to stress at the outset that the strongest argument for raising the ethics bar boils down to self-interest. I believe that good business ethics is good for the bottom line and good for shareholder value.

As corporations, we live at the sufferance of the public. If we don't behave well, we can be regulated, we can be sued, all sorts of bad things can happen to us. And everyday, it seems, yet another company is the subject of the "wrong kind" of story in the *Wall Street Journal.* Stories about sexual harassment, environmental contamination, antitrust infractions, illegal foreign payments, fraudu-

Excerpted from "Business Ethics and Corporate Responsibility: Good for the Bottom Line," by Stephen Butler, speech given to recognize 100 Florida companies, February 28, 1997, Orlando, FL. Reprinted with permission.

lent financial reporting and race issues. Today, companies cannot afford negative publicity. Loss of confidence in an organization is the single greatest cost of unethical behavior. Once the media gets hold of that story, your customers will avoid you like the plague. An essential part of an ethics process is identifying issues that would mortify a chief executive if he were to read about them on the front page of the newspapers.

"Good ethics means good business."

What it all translates into is this. We live in a time when the ill considered actions of a handful of employees can suddenly reverse years of effort to build a solid corporate name.

And I'm saying this because I really believe that corporate ethics are essential for a successful business today and the CEOs of corporate America are the only ones who can institutionalize it.

I'm not a scholar in the field of ethics, or a person uniquely qualified to explore the subject. . . . I am a businessman like most of you and by choice, a leader. And although I think the thousands of people who work for KPMG believe I lead with a degree of vision, I know I lead mostly with common sense.

Common sense dictates many of the decisions I make both large and small. However, there's a problem with common sense. What I may think is pure, unadulterated common sense, someone else may not. So if we business leaders rely on the common sense of our co-workers to act in an ethical manner, it simply won't happen as we imagine and even expect it to. We can't take ethics for granted assuming that problems only happen to the other guy.

Judging Corporate Character

People already judge the worth of my company and yours, not just by our bottom line, but by the contents of our corporate character. They judge our employees not just by their work product. Is it enough to have the cheapest shirt or the cheapest pair of pants sitting on the store shelves? Ask those companies that have been publicly flogged for supplying the competitively priced goods that we demand, that were sewn together in sweatshops or by child labor making pennies a day.

On the other hand, take a look at Johnson & Johnson—a company that is the hallmark of American corporate ethics. Their code of ethics is a part of the very fabric of the company reaching as far back as the mid '40s. In the 1980s, J&J's response to not one but two Tylenol tragedies [when bottles of Tylenol were discovered to contain lethal doses of cyanide] and its subsequent media exposure etched in the public's collective mind the reputation of Johnson & Johnson as the company to trust.

By voluntarily pulling massive amounts of at-risk product immediately off the shelf, J&J proved that its corporate decision making was driven by what was ethical, not expedient. But were their actions good business? You judge.

Within days of the second Tylenol tragedy their stock actually climbed ten points, with analysts attributing the rise to the company's speedy and ethical crisis response. . . .

Instituting a corporate ethics program in an organization isn't a matter of religion. It isn't a spiritual issue, not even strictly a legal or regulatory issue. It's simply the right thing to do. And in the long haul, companies will and do profit from having and enforcing strong ethics programs.

But what is the definition of ethics? According to the dictionary, ethics is a system of moral principles or values.

For me, the answer is simpler. Evil people will do whatever they want one way or another. That bad people do bad things is uncontrollable. Ethics means making sure good people don't do bad things, intentionally or unintentionally. But the evidence is mounting that much of the time the employees who engage in the most damaging misconduct are basically good people who think they are doing what their company really wants. The goal of business ethics is to keep good people from lapsing, or from looking the other way.

Mixed Signals

Serious problems most typically arise when people feel incented or pressured to do things they shouldn't. One study, published by the California Management Review in January 1995, looked at the first five years after graduation and employment of 30 Harvard University MBA graduates. Twenty-nine of them said that business pressures had forced them to violate their own personal ethical standards.

People tend to do what they perceive their company, manager or supervisor wants them to do. And based on their work environment or culture, people usually decide what it takes to be successful, then go in that direction. To me that means there are a lot of mixed signals being sent. Do we want our employees to be ethical or are we signaling them to do whatever it takes to just get it done? The message is pointedly driven home to them in performance evaluations, pay raises, promotions, and not so subtle reminders that others can do their job if they "can't cut it."

"Good business ethics is good for the bottom line and good for shareholder value."

At the same time they are vaguely aware of a company code of conduct that tells them to act honestly and they have also received some training.

Too often they resolve these two seemingly competing messages in favor of the business goal, because they hear that message more loudly than the ethics message. They keep their heads down and quietly do what they assume is what the company really wants them to do: just get it done, whatever it takes.

Ethics programs must be more than window dressing that creates a paper trail to cover our behinds. Our role as leaders is to set the tone at the top by

Executives Are Not Overcompensated

Holman W. Jenkins Jr.

About the author: *Holman W. Jenkins Jr. is a business reporter and columnist* [for] *the Wall Street Journal.*

Since the takeover battles of the 1980s, the media has befuddled itself over the emergence of ever-fatter CEO salaries, golden parachutes and other large individual payments, which have become the norm in corporate restructuring dramas. These are seen as evidence of market failure—i.e., CEOs are looting—or as proof that the rich are only getting richer, while everybody else gets laid off.

A Way to Balance Powerful Egos

It seems to have occurred to only a few eccentric economists that, in the field of human conflict, money's growing role as the universal solvent actually represents progress. If golden parachutes had existed in Shakespeare's day, the bard would have had fewer regicides, parricides and fratricides to dramatize.

By contrast, where in centuries past they might have solved their problems by slaughtering each other, the feuding barons of Time Warner were handed bucks totaling an estimated $120 million to take themselves out of the picture [so] King Gerald [CEO Gerald Levin] could assert some mastery over the flailing entertainment giant. Or consider a counterexample: the scuttled merger between two big California HMOs, Wellpoint and Health Systems, a deal that Wall Street professed to love. Neither side's management could agree on who would be in charge and fell to bickering over the size of each other's severance contracts. But many shareholders might have been willing to sweeten the parachutes if that would have encouraged one management or the other to take early retirement.

There's no getting around the fact that change brings powerful egos and interests into conflict. This is especially so in the swaths of corporate America that are being transformed by technology and deregulation, like health care, banking, telecommunications and entertainment. In just these areas, compensation

---

building incentives that advance good business practices without sacrificing incentives that drive the bottom line. If we can instill an unbending belief in our work force that ethics is "simply the way we do business," our employees will instinctively resist courses of action that can lastingly tarnish our company's reputation.

Unfortunately, there's more talk than action these days with "Corporate Conscience" awards literally being bestowed for intentions only. A consumer organization, the Council on Economic Priorities, awarded Starbucks its annual prize despite grassroots protests against the coffee retailer's labor practices. Starbucks was sourcing beans from export houses that pay Guatemalan workers about $2.50 per day. When asked why Starbucks was honored, the Executive Vice President of the Council was quoted saying, "their mission statement alone, was enough to earn Starbucks the honor."

> "Instituting a corporate ethics program in an organization . . . is simply the right thing to do."

Socially responsible business is not about a company's intentions. And when noble posturing is rewarded, the need for action is seriously diluted. Mission statements aren't enough. They're merely a start.

Don't be sucked in by words in place of actions. Because without a viable action plan, a code of ethics is little more than balm to soothe our internal and external constituencies.

Implementing Ethical Practices

So let's talk implementation and accountability. This is the most difficult part.

According to the ethics officer of a multi-billion dollar pharmaceutical company, his company has what he calls a "state-of-the-art" ethics program including a "zero tolerance" policy. If someone is found to be involved in an antitrust situation, sexual harassment or even cheating on an expense report, they're gone.

And one of the fundamentals of the program is even-handed application at every level of the corporation—no double standard. If it's only going to be enforced at lower levels, letting errant executives off the hook, "the program has no credibility."

Take for example, the storm of criticism over the U.S. Army's latest sexual harassment scandal. Though its top enlisted soldier was charged with sexually harassing a former subordinate, he was allowed to continue his day-to-day duties. At lower levels, soldiers charged with similar transgressions had been suspended immediately. Media pressure and public outcries ultimately forced even-handed application. But the cost to the Army has been a major disruption in its recruitment efforts.

At the heart of every program, there must be openness. If your employees won't turn in violators because they're afraid of retaliation, good people become numb to questionable practices or they become frustrated and leave. . . .

Ethics programs benefit organizations of all shapes and sizes. Take, for example, a small, privately held real estate company in North Carolina. It specializes in managing low-income housing in the rural Southeast.

For several years, it has had an ethics code which all 150 managers and supervisors are required to sign annually. In 1996, a sexual harassment charge was leveled by an employee against a property manager.

Both had read and signed the ethics code months before the alleged incident occurred. When the existence of the signed code of ethics was brought to the forefront, the company was absolved of any wrongdoing and charges against it dropped. The real estate firm's proactive stance saved it significant costs and valuable time and energy, and possible damage to its reputation.

Avoiding Penalties

Though the outcome was positive, even good rules can't always guarantee ethical conduct and when bad things happen, the Federal Government may end up dictating the results. Unless you've been unconscious for the past several years, it would be difficult not to know about the Federal Sentencing Guidelines and about the staggering penalties levied for corporate misconduct. Record-breaking fines and an unprecedented new sanction called "corporate probation" have wreaked havoc on several major corporations.

And if you're imagining that corporate probation is a slap on the wrist, forget it! It means a court-appointed monitor will roam completely without restraint around your company. They can talk freely to your employees, examine your books and records, and report any violation of the law to the court. And that's on your nickel, by the way. Then it's your responsibility to convince the court to make the monitor go away.

Now if that concept has you sweating, the new penalty scheme has its pluses for organizations with strong ethics and compliance programs. Notice I said those corporations that backed words with actions. Even if someone within your ranks does something seriously wrong, with an ethics program in place you'll have a nearly air-tight defense against the most severe penalties. Essen-

> *"The goal of business ethics is to keep good [employees] from lapsing, or from looking the other way."*

tially, the new law is an incentive to take compliance and ethics seriously.

But this is only the beginning of the story because the same reduced liability approach is showing up in other legal areas like the Department of Health and Human Services and the Justice Department's Criminal and Environmental Divisions. Both have indicated that a company's risk of even being prosecuted will sharply decline in proportion to the strength of its ethics and compliance commitment.

Building an Ethical Stand

Our employees must have clear knowledge of the dards and equally important, a feeling of managem within those standards. The American public can't af to be considered an oxymoron.

One so-called expert suggested recently in the *Wall*

> *"Ethics programs must be more than window dressing that creates a paper trail to cover our behinds."*

to save ou tion by forb of meeting shredding decisions. I there's some One of the

sibilities we as business leaders have today is to provi which our employees, customers and suppliers view a duct. The challenge for each of us is to avoid creatin standards and instead, build the real thing! If we're on should demand the same of those businesses. When we trickle down to the bottom line; they'll flow.

guru Graef Crystal finds CEO salaries running 40% to 80% above the norm for more sedentary industries. Anecdotally, these are often the same businesses where we see large side payments being spread among leading personalities in order to bring off new business combinations and structures.

Time Warner is the most interesting, if extreme, case. CEO Gerald Levin oversees a massive collection of disparate entertainment assets, faces a puzzle in how to organize these elements and make them pay off for shareholders in the multimedia future, and has to act quickly before the owners throw him out. Whatever plan he dreams up is bound to run up against the ambitions and obstinacy of a lot of powerful colleagues. He might sit down and reason with each one, or alternatively take them to court. But the quickest way to the heart of any matter is with a big check.

So, along with buying out his stake in Turner Broadcasting, Ted Turner has been guaranteed $100 million in cash personally for merging with Time Warner and, presumably, to soothe him into the unaccustomed role of underling. Likewise, John Malone, one of Mr. Turner's biggest shareholders and a potential monkey wrench in the deal, was given an unprecedented 20 years of discount programming (conservatively estimated at $500 million) for his cable network. Last but not least, Mike Milken reportedly was to earn $50 million for five days of doing whatever voodoo he did to bring these formidable parties into line.

Mr. Levin has also spent a fortune in shareholder money to resolve the internal rivalries bedeviling his game plan for Time Warner. Robert Morgado, the head of Warner Music, pushed out lieutenants Mo Ostin, Lenny Waronker and Bob Krasnow, who reportedly got severance worth tens of millions; then Mr. Morgado himself was pushed out by Michael Fuchs, brought over from HBO to run the combined music and studio operations. In one report, Mr. Morgado got $40 million. A few months later, Mr. Fuchs was out with a fat parachute of his own.

In total, Time Warner is expected to spend about $120 million to cushion the fall of its internal titans, plus several hundred million more to bring outsiders like Messrs. Turner and Malone into conformity with the CEO's strategy. This is expensive, but not as expensive as piddling around. In a world where capital deserts a loser in a heartbeat, time is the only thing Mr. Levin can't afford.

Are shareholders outraged by these payments? It doesn't seem so. Few CEOs in America are more hectored by big-time investors, but the market's generally approving take seems to be that Mr. Levin is finally beginning to get his hands around the

> *"All the evidence is that increased managerial accountability lies behind the big-bucks phenomenon."*

tiller. Indeed, management is expected to tap the kitty again soon to buy off US West's opposition to the Turner deal (the Baby Bell owns a chunk of Time Warner's movie and cable operations and is suing to block the merger). If Time

Warner's stock has been faltering of late, the reason may be the one pothole that greenmail won't pave over—the federal antitrust bureaucracy.

Worth the Expense

Not everybody is happy with the trend toward large payments to individuals, since it reflects capitalism's habit of making money the mediator in more and more human relationships, rather than, say, noblesse oblige or legal prescription. But all the evidence is that increased managerial accountability lies behind the big-bucks phenomenon. In corporate life no less than in other realms, there is endless scope for the messy play of ego, ambition and personal irascibility. Large sums of money are great simplifiers and clarifiers.

Nowhere is this clearer than in involuntary management changes, where a big enough severance check can help even the most egocentric CEO see how it might serve shareholders if he made himself scarce. In 1995, Kmart CEO Joseph Antonini, a lifelong employee, finally walked the plank with an estimated $5 million lifevest; happy shareholders bid up the company's value by nearly $500 million in a single day. Mickey Schulhof, head of Sony's spendthrift, rudderless and foundering U.S. operations, fell on his sword in December 1995 with a severance deal of undoubtedly grand dimensions. Not known for humility, Mr. Schulhof humbly cited the right of Sony's Japanese chairman to appoint somebody whose "style" he was more comfortable with.

> *"An underpaid CEO is likely to be an overcautious one."*

For people who worry about the power of money, it ought to be reassuring to see human capital getting the best of mere financial capital, which is what many of these cases are about. It should also comfort to recognize that, in the final analysis, these sums are operating to purify decision-making. As Sherry Lansing, head of Paramount Pictures, explained to the *New York Times*, an underpaid CEO is likely to be an overcautious one: "The only way you can perform in a job is if you don't need it."

Chapter 3

Are Modern Biomedical Practices Ethical?

Chapter Preface

In recent years, society has witnessed an explosion of medical and biotechnological advances. Medical procedures that were innovative only a few decades ago—such as organ transplants and in-vitro fertilization—now seem ordinary and commonplace. More recently, scientists have been making significant discoveries in areas that once were relegated to the world of science fiction, including cloning and genetic engineering.

However, many of these biomedical advances raise serious ethical questions. For example, successes in cloning animals have sparked such controversy over the imminent possibility of cloning humans that the U.S. government has placed a moratorium on federally funded research into human cloning. In ordering the ban, President Bill Clinton asserted, "Any discovery that touches upon human creation is not simply a matter of scientific inquiry. It is a matter of morality and spirituality as well."

Opponents of human cloning fear that the procedure will be used in unethical ways. They argue, for instance, that a clone might be produced to serve as an "organ bank" for an individual in need of a transplant. According to Kevin T. Fitzgerald, a professor in molecular genetics, "Cloning a human being solely for the purpose of supplying organs or tissue makes it, at a minimum, a mere instrument for manipulation and negates the human identity of the clone." Other critics maintain that the negation of human identity will be a factor even in clones who are created for more ethical reasons. They insist that cloned humans will suffer from the knowledge that they are "copies" of another person rather than unique individuals.

On the other hand, supporters of human cloning contend that the potential benefits of the procedure far outweigh the concerns expressed by critics. These advocates assert that cloning will provide hope to infertile couples who have not been able to conceive children by any other means. Although each clone will share the same genetic makeup as another individual, they maintain, a clone will still have its own unique personality. Ronald Bailey, a contributing editor for *Reason* magazine, points out that identical twins also share the same genes, yet "no one has argued that twins are immoral." Unethical uses of human cloning can be prohibited while still allowing the procedure for beneficial purposes, advocates conclude.

Even as the controversy around human cloning rages, scientists continue to announce new breakthroughs that lead to more ethical debates. The following chapter explores the ethical dilemmas surrounding human cloning and other modern biomedical practices.

Cloning Is Ethical

by Ronald Bailey

About the author: *Ronald Bailey is a writer and television producer in Washington, D.C., and a contributing editor to* Reason *magazine.*

Cloning human cells could one day save your life and the lives of the people you love. Yet Congress seems hellbent on stopping the medical advances that cloning can make possible. Congress is responding to polls that show most Americans are opposed to the cloning of human beings. But carelessly crafted legislation would restrict not only research leading to the birth of cloned people but research that could find cures for cancer, genetic diseases such as cystic fibrosis, and damaged hearts, livers, and brains. . . .

Society's Reaction to a Cloning Breakthrough

In February 1997, the Roslin Institute in Scotland, an obscure farm animal research facility, announced that it had succeeded in cloning a sheep from an adult, differentiated cell. The cloned sheep, Dolly, made headlines around the world and launched a fierce debate over the potential uses for this new technology. The breakthrough showed for the first time that genetic information encoded in the DNA of an adult cell could be "reset" and made young again. Once reset, the cells with rejuvenated DNA could produce all of the cells needed to grow a complete organism. "[S]uperficially, it's a step toward immortality," explained Ronald James, whose company, PPL Therapeutics, paid for the cloning research. "And if you take a step toward immortality, everybody stops and takes notice."

Since Dolly, much has happened. President Bill Clinton imposed a ban on federally funded cloning research, and Pope John Paul II declared that each human being has a "right to a unique human genome." UNESCO has issued a Universal Declaration on the Human Genome and Human Rights declaring, "Practices which are contrary to human dignity, such as reproductive cloning of human beings, shall not be permitted." The European Union has also adopted a ban.

In the United States, the National Bioethics Advisory Commission issued a report in June 1997 calling for federal legislation to ban human cloning for three to five years. "Freelance" physicist Richard Seed created a mini media firestorm in December 1997 when he said he was looking for investors to open a cloning clinic. Congressional hearings have been held, and in February 1998 the U.S. Senate debated a bill that would ban cloning research on human embryos. Throughout it all, bioethicists have been offering grim warnings about the moral dangers of human cloning.

> *"Cloning techniques could be the basis for a variety of life-saving medical treatments."*

As *New York Times* science reporter Gina Kolata shows in her book *Clone: The Road to Dolly and the Path Ahead*, the science of cloning is fascinating. The achievement of Ian Wilmut and his colleagues at the Roslin Institute was the culmination of decades of research on eggs, embryos, and in vitro fertilization. The researchers inserted the nucleus of an adult udder cell into a sheep egg cell whose nucleus had been removed, a technique called "somatic cell nuclear transfer." Once the egg with its new nucleus began to divide, Wilmut implanted the developing embryo into the uterus of another sheep, the surrogate mother who gave birth to Dolly.

Potential Medical Benefits

If it can be done with sheep, there appears to be no biological reason it cannot be done with human beings. Putting that possibility aside, however, cloning techniques could be the basis for a variety of life-saving medical treatments. Cloning probably will first be used to create animals that excrete important therapeutic human proteins, such as insulin or interferons, in their milk. This is what Wilmut was trying to do.

Another exciting possibility is that doctors, using somatic cell nuclear transfer, could create embryonic stem (ES) cells, the self-renewing precursors to blood, skin, heart, and nerve cells.

The treatment for leukemia, a cancer in which the bone marrow overproduces white blood cells, could be revolutionized. Today, one of the more successful treatments involves the destruction of a patient's bone marrow through chemotherapy and the transplantation of healthy marrow cells taken from a closely matched donor. The problem is that many leukemia patients die because they can't find appropriate donors. With cloning, healthy marrow cells that are perfect genetic matches for a leukemia patient could be created from the patient's own cells. Doctors could take a skin cell nucleus and implant it in an enucleated human egg, resetting the cell's DNA. Once reset, the cell could become an embryonic stem cell. After the ES cells began to divide, they could be treated with hormones that would cause them to develop into marrow cells, which could then be returned to the patient.

Similarly, islet cells could be created from the skin cells of a diabetic and returned to the patient's pancreas, where they would produce insulin. Eventually,

ES cells could be turned into healthy heart or liver cells that could be used to repair tissue damaged by heart attacks or hepatitis.

Congress is considering several bills, sponsored mainly by Republicans, that would ban the research that could lead to these new treatments. Stampeded by the anti-abortion lobby, congressional Republicans want to treat ES cells like human embryos, even though their ultimate form depends entirely on the intentions of the patients and doctors who create them.

In his book *Remaking Eden: Cloning and Beyond in a Brave New World*, Princeton University science professor Lee Silver highlights the important distinction between growth and development. ES cells can grow and divide into millions of identical cells, but they do not develop into any particular kind of cell until told to do so through biochemical signals. In a sense, the creation of ES cells in vitro would be like enhancing the natural production of ES cells in vivo. ES cells created from a patient's skin to treat disease are no more ethically problematic than veins taken from his legs to be used in a heart bypass operation. Both are the patient's cells, and both are being used for purposes different from their original function.

Down the road, it may be possible to reset cells without using enucleated human ova. Scientists in Wisconsin are doing some promising work using cow eggs to rejuvenate DNA taken from other species. But right now, researchers need to use human eggs in order to learn about the process of re-

> *"If research . . . is blocked, . . . many people who might have lived will die."*

setting cells. Such knowledge could lead to cures for cancer by teaching doctors how to turn off the uncontrolled growth of cancer cells, avoiding the relatively crude radiation and chemotherapy treatments used today. If research using human ova is blocked, the development of new treatments will be delayed, and many people who might have lived will die.

Human Cloning

But what about cloning a complete human being? This prospect seems to cause the greatest unease among bioethicists and the general public, but it's not clear exactly why. A clone would be a delayed identical twin of the person from whom the cell's nucleus was taken. A clone is therefore a human being with all of the rights and responsibilities of any other human being. "How could we expect God to treat anyone born through cloning any different from the rest of us?" asks Ted Peters, a fellow at the Center for Theology and the Natural Sciences and a professor at Pacific Lutheran Seminary. "Surely, they would be just as much a child of God and loved by God. They would have their individuality, they would have their dignity, and certainly they would have their own souls."

The National Bioethics Advisory Commission suggested that human cloning be banned for three to five years on the grounds that it is not yet "safe" for the children who might be born using the procedure. The commission based its decision on the fact that Dolly was born after 277 attempts, which it argued is too high a failure rate when applied to human cloning. But is it really?

Lee Silver notes that hundreds of human eggs and embryos were used before the birth of the first test-tube baby, Louise Joy Brown, in 1978. Dolly was actually the beneficiary of well-established human in vitro fertilization technology: In the 277 tries, only 29 of the fused udder cells actually became embryos, which were implanted in 13 ewes, of which one became pregnant and gave birth. In a sense, this was a perfect success rate, since the only pregnancy resulted in a healthy birth. It is certainly far superior to the success rates achieved in early human IVF efforts. Silver claims that reproductive human cloning is no more dangerous than current human IVF procedures, which result in fewer birth defects than do natural births. An estimated 150,000 test-tube babies have been born worldwide.

Many of the same bioethicists who decried test-tube babies, including Leon Kass of the University of Chicago and Daniel Callahan of the Hastings Institute, are in the forefront of the attempts to ban human cloning. Twenty years ago, these bioluddites portentously warned that test-tube babies would break the natural bonds of family, with unimaginable consequences for society. Although their warnings have proven unjustified, the naysayers are dusting off the old arguments and applying them to this new advance.

The National Bioethics Advisory Commission correctly refused to take a stand on the morality of human cloning, noting our society's diversity of values. The pope is free to advise Roman Catholics about what he believes the proper way to reproduce is, but his values are not universal.

The commission could not find a secular basis for banning the cloning of human beings. After all, who would be hurt by cloning? The person being cloned? Not if he gives permission. The baby? There is little reason to believe that "unnatural" methods of reproduction are any more harmful to offspring than the usual way of having children. There is no evidence, for example, that test-tube babies suffer especially high rates of physical or psychological problems.

Try this thought experiment. If tomorrow someone could prove that you were a clone, would you think your life was worth less, that your loves and experiences were devalued? You would be the same person you always were. Nothing would be different simply because you were born from a "previously experienced genome," in the tortured language of the cloning prohibitionists. A clone would likely have no more issues about self-worth and life chances than test-tube babies or adopted children do today.

> *"A clone is . . . a human being with all of the rights and responsibilities of any other human being."*

One often hears that cloning will bring on Aldous Huxley's *Brave New World*.

But that is nonsense. Huxley's dystopia was a centrally planned world in which clones were created by the state. In our society, choices will and should be made by individuals who are helping their children have a better life. One day, cloning technology probably will make possible changes in the genomes of embryos. Parents who risk having children with genetic diseases will be able to have the DNA of their prospective children repaired at the embryo stage, protecting them against maladies such as cystic fibrosis, PKU, and Tay-Sachs. A further benefit is that their grandchildren will never contract these diseases.

> *"There is little reason to believe that 'unnatural' methods of reproduction are . . . harmful to offspring."*

Parents will not only be able to prevent disease, they may also be able to enhance their children. Parents invest a lot of time, money, and emotional energy in providing good health care and a solid education for their children. If, by tweaking a base pair or two in a child's DNA, parents could boost the kid's intelligence and ensure against genetic diseases, what's so wrong with that? More to the point, who has the right to stop them?

"We control all other aspects of our children's lives and identities through powerful social and environmental influences and, in some cases, with the use of powerful drugs like Ritalin and Prozac," notes Silver. "On what basis can we reject positive genetic influences on a person's essence when we accept the rights of parents to benefit their children in every other way?"

Opponents of cloning talk a lot about hubris. But it takes more than a little hubris to believe you are wise enough to tell other people what is best for them—which is, after all, what a ban on cloning amounts to. What about the human consequences of banning a technology—the death, disease, disability, indignity, unhappiness, and blighted lives that would result from imposing limits on cloning discoveries and advances? Trying to exercise prior restraint on scientific and medical research is fraught with moral peril. Cloning prohibitionists must be held responsible for preventing the discovery of a cure for AIDS, cancer, Tays-Sachs, or heart disease. Their efforts to ban cloning could stop the creation of new medicines that would help millions of people.

Questions of Risk and Dignity

Some opponents of cloning say it is too risky. But what opponents of a new technology regard as too risky may be acceptable for others. After all, some people parachute out of airplanes, while others won't even ride jetliners. "Risk" is not an objective quality of an object or technology; it is inextricably tied up with one's values. Why should cloning opponents get to impose their values on sick or dying people?

With regard to the perennial argument that cloning might violate "human dignity," bioethicist Ruth Macklin of Albert Einstein Medical College rightly observes that people who are worried about this issue "owe us a more precise account of just what constitutes a violation of human dignity if no one's rights are violated. Dignity is a fuzzy concept and appeals to dignity are often used to substitute for empirical evidence that is lacking or sound arguments that cannot be mustered." After all, what is so dignified about dying of cystic fibrosis, diabetes, or cancer? . . .

Will Needed Research Be Hampered?

Twenty-five years ago, bioluddites tried to stop recombinant DNA research, the technique which allows scientists to swap genes from one organism to another. Today Nobel laureate James Watson, the co-discoverer of the structure of DNA, is worried about the new assault on biotechnological progress. "Ever since we achieved a breakthrough in the area of recombinant DNA in 1973, left-wing nuts and environmental kooks have been screaming that we will create some kind of Frankenstein bug or Andromeda strain that will destroy us all," Watson tells Kolata. "Now we are threatened with a truly imbecilic law that could set back research for years." Kolata notes that "the transformation of recombinant DNA from the greatest threat since the atom bomb to a tool for the pharmaceutical industry occurred with little comment."

"If tomorrow someone could prove that you were a clone, would you think your life was worth less?"

"Human essence came into existence simply because those with it could out-compete and kill those without it," writes Silver. "But if human minds have the ability to contemplate and direct changes in the copies of their own genomes that they give to future generations, the human mind is much more than the genes that brought it into existence." Let's hope that humanity will not shrink from using this promising new brainchild, continuing what Francis Bacon called "the conquest of nature for the relief of man's estate."

Human Stem Cell Research Is Ethical

by Lawrence S.B. Goldstein

About the author: *Lawrence S.B. Goldstein is an investigator for the Howard Hughes Medical Institute and a professor in the division of cellular and molecular medicine and the department of pharmacology at the University of California in San Diego.*

Why should we use federal funds for human pluripotent stem cell research? Ask [former pro football player] Walter Payton and 12,000 other Americans who are waiting for liver transplants. If they are fortunate, new livers will be found and they may live; if not, they will die. [Editor's note: Walter Payton died of liver cancer on November 1, 1999.]

Ask my friend Doug, who has a 7-year-old son with diabetes. Every night he and his wife are awake in the wee hours, monitoring their son's blood, worrying that they have missed the balance and that their beloved child will slip into a coma.

Ask the children of millions more like them, for whom insulin is a treatment but not a cure, because crucial cells in the pancreas are still missing. These children are always in danger, and they live under the constant shadow of premature death or disability.

The Need for Research

New hope for these desperately ill people has come from the recent discovery of "human pluripotent stem cells," the primordial cells from which all the tissues and organs of the body develop. However, a serious debate has erupted on Capitol Hill about whether federal funds should be used to support further research in this area. At issue is whether the merits of public funding and the dreadful burden of disease balance concerns about the origin of these special cells.

To understand the need for research with human pluripotent stem cells, one need look no further than many common diseases such as cancer, heart disease and kidney disease. These diseases are treatable in whole or in part by tissue or

Reprinted from "Providing Hope Through Stem Cell Research," by Lawrence S.B. Goldstein, *San Diego Union-Tribune,* May 25, 1999. Reprinted with permission from the author.

organ transplants, but there are persistent and deadly problems of rejection and a completely inadequate supply of suitable donor organs and tissues.

In addition, the grim arithmetic of most organ transplants is that those who are seriously ill wait for the tragic accidental death of another person so that they may live. Worse, for juvenile diabetes and many other diseases, there is not even a suitable transplantation therapy or other cure.

> *"Federal funding is the best way to guarantee that stem cell therapies are developed with the greatest consideration of the public good."*

The recent discovery of human pluripotent stem cells has suddenly given us the potential to escape these dilemmas and provide our most desperately ill children, friends, parents and neighbors with new tissues and organs to replace their own damaged ones. Pluripotent human stem cells, unlike all other cells in the human body, seem to "remember" how to become almost any type of cell or organ.

Our scientists are at the threshold of learning how to coax these cells into growing into the many kinds of organs and tissues needed by our gravely ill citizens, without the potential problems of rejection seen in most transplants. Thus, our researchers may soon be able to generate pancreatic cells to save my friend Doug's son, and liver cells to rescue Walter Payton and those like him.

Possible treatments for Alzheimer's disease and many cancers may also be forthcoming. Federal funding for research with pluripotent human stem cells is desperately needed for our scientists and physicians to realize these worthy goals.

Although human pluripotent stem cell research has tremendous medical potential, some of our citizens and legislators seek to prohibit our best and brightest federally funded university scientists and physicians from working with human pluripotent stem cells. They do so because of ethical concerns about the origins of these cells, which were derived from the earliest human blastocyst stage embryos.

While I, and many other scientists, share these concerns, we believe that the potential benefit of such work and other ethical considerations balance the concerns about the origins of these cells. In fact, 33 Nobel laureates recently wrote to the president and the Congress in support of federal funding for research with human pluripotent stem cells to ensure that those with deadly diseases are given this chance.

Federal Funding and Ethical Research

There are several major reasons to believe that federal support of human pluripotent stem cell research is both appropriate and ethical:

• Using federal funds to support pluripotent stem cell research guarantees proper ethical oversight and public input into this important work. Federal funding of this research will require the scientific community and the government to work together to establish an appropriate set of rules for this research. These rules will ensure the advancement of critical medical research and maintain respect for public sensibilities.

The National Institutes of Health has already developed an outline of such a system. For federally funded research, this system will prohibit the use of pluripotent stem cells that have come from "embryo farms" or from embryos purchased or sold, and will continue to ensure that human embryos are not created for research purposes. It will also continue to be illegal to use federal funds to derive pluripotent stem cells from human embryos.

• Banning federal funding for human pluripotent stem cell research will not eliminate it. Such research will proceed in private industry and in other countries. This fact prompts serious concern that the work may then be conducted in secret, without the benefit of ethical regulation or public debate as it proceeds.

• Using federal funds for human pluripotent stem cell research ensures that our best and most capable scientists will participate in this research. Without such funding, new treatments will be delayed by years, and

> *"Should we not use cells derived from donated embryos to save lives?"*

many who might otherwise have been saved will surely die or endure needless suffering.

• Federal funding is the best way to guarantee that stem cell therapies are developed with the greatest consideration of the public good. In the absence of federal funding, it is likely that stem-cell derived treatments will only be found for diseases that commercial companies determine will yield the largest profit if treated. Thus, market forces could create a situation where deadly, but less profitable, diseases are ignored.

No Other Ethical Use

• Although it is essential that we use federal funds to support pluripotent stem cell research, the stem cells themselves will be derived without using federal funds from early embryos that are destined to be discarded. In vitro fertilization treatments for childless couples often produce more embryos than can be implanted into the mother. These embryos cannot develop on their own, have only a few cells, and must either be stored in freezers indefinitely, or eventually destroyed.

There is no other ethical use for these embryos if the parents choose not to have them implanted into the mother. Even if one believes that the destruction of these embryos is a tragedy, should we not allow the parents the right to make the decision to donate them for pluripotent stem cell derivation and stem cell research so that many other people might live? Should we not use cells derived from donated embryos to save lives, just as we do after an auto accident by using the organs of those who tragically died?

• Balancing the ethical objections of some to pluripotent stem cell research are the serious ethical implications of not proceeding. Can we justify turning our backs on our children, parents and friends who will suffer and die if we do not find suitable cures? Ethically validated pluripotent stem cell research provides new hope for these people.

In the past few years, Congress has wisely and dramatically increased federal funding for biomedical research. We must ensure that these funds are used for the best and most promising medical research.

Ethics, scientific opportunity and medical need can surely be balanced. Ask Walter Payton or my friend Doug if you're still not sure.

Allowing the Sale of Human Organs Could Be Ethical

by Pete du Pont

About the author: *Formerly the governor of Delaware, Pete du Pont is the policy chairman for the National Center for Policy Analysis, a public policy research institute headquartered in Dallas, Texas.*

There are currently about 45,000 people waiting for a human organ transplant. About 3,000 of them will die on that waiting list because a suitable transplant organ will not become available in time.

The short supply of organs has recently led to some overt attempts to ration them in a way that would be more beneficial to society. For example, the United Network for Organ Sharing has altered its guidelines for those needing a liver transplant so that those with acute liver problems get priority. Those with a chronic liver condition like hepatitis or cirrhosis (which could be the result of alcohol abuse) cannot rise above the second level in priority status.

The legislature in the state of Washington recently passed a measure—which the governor vetoed for being too vague—that would prohibit those on Death Row from receiving "lifesaving health care procedures" such as an organ transplant.

Now the Cleveland Clinic is being accused of removing organs before some patients are legally dead.

Instead of looking for new ways to ration organs or take them prematurely, we should ask how we can increase the supply of organs so that doctors are not forced to decide who lives and who dies.

Compensating Donors

The answer is to compensate donors for their organs. Unfortunately, doing so is currently against the law. That's because the National Organ Transplant Act (1984) prohibits "any person to knowingly acquire, receive or otherwise trans-

Reprinted from "Market Card for Organ Donors?" by Pete du Pont, *The Washington Times,* October 2, 1997. Reprinted with permission from the author.

fer any human organ for valuable consideration for use in human transplantation." As a result, altruism is the only legal motive for individuals or their surrogates to donate their organs.

But while altruism is a noble motive, it is seldom a compelling one. Economic theory clearly recognizes that when demand for a good or service is high, its price will increase until the supply and demand reach an equilibrium. If the price is prohibited from rising, a shortage will occur because people will not provide a product when the price is too low. Thus, permitting donors to receive some type of compensation for their organs would help alleviate our organ-shortage problem.

Opponents of a market for organs immediately conjure up images of strange people selling off body parts. But a market for organs could develop in a number of ways: Some would be more open and direct, while others might be indirect and incorporate the concerns of some of those who oppose compensation.

We could, for example, permit a donor pool. Dr. Robert M. Sade, a surgeon and professor of medicine at the Medical University of South Carolina, and his colleagues have proposed creating an in-kind market for organs. Every adult would be given the option of joining the Transplant Recipient and Donor Organization. Membership would require permission to have your organs removed at death, and only those joining would be permitted to receive a transplanted organ. Those who chose not to join would be electing for standard medical care, short of transplantation. Thus, the only way to receive an organ while living would be to have given permission to have your organs taken at death.

> *"Permitting donors to receive some type of compensation for their organs would help alleviate our organ-shortage problem."*

Permit people to receive after-death compensation. A person wanting to become an organ donor would simply contract with an organ-donor organization, which would compensate the deceased's estate for each organ successfully harvested. The compensation could be in a variety of forms. A hospital or organ-donor network might pay part or all of a donor's burial expenses, for example. Such a provision might encourage lower-income people who could not afford life insurance to sign up for the program as a way to provide for their funeral costs. (A similar provision has been supported by an article in the *Journal of the American Medical Association*.)

Or contribute funds to the donor's designated charity—a hospital, university or social services agency. Let people sell whatever they want, when they want. The most open and market-oriented approach would be to let anyone who wanted to sell one or more organs do so. Thus, if someone needed a kidney and was willing to pay for one, a compatible donor could provide the recipient with a kidney for the market-set price.

A variation on this proposal would let people sell their organs now at a discounted price for harvesting after death.

Creating More Choices

There are obvious dangers in this approach that would need more thought before it is adopted. The pressures on people unable to make knowledgeable decisions might be prohibitive.

The point is, there are ways to encourage people to donate their organs to help others live. These mechanisms would increase the supply of organs, the waiting lines and needless deaths would decrease, if not disappear, and donors and recipients would have more choices.

While opponents to these proposals want more organs, they don't want a market for organs. Paternalistically, they impose their values on everyone else. And with regard to organ availability, while paternalism lives, people die.

Cloning Is Unethical

by Leon R. Kass

About the author: *A physician and biochemist, Leon R. Kass is the Addie Clark Harding Professor in the Committee on Social Thought and the College of the University of Chicago. He is the coauthor of* The Ethics of Human Cloning *and the author of* Toward a More Natural Science: Biology and Human Affairs.

Editor's Note: The following viewpoint was originally presented as testimony before the National Bioethics Advisory Commission, which was directed by President Bill Clinton to review the implications of cloning humans. In June 1997, the commission recommended that research into human cloning be banned for three to five years.

I am deeply grateful for the opportunity to present some of my thoughts about the ethics of human cloning, by which I mean precisely the production of cloned human beings.

This topic has occupied me off and on for over 30 years; it was the subject of one of my first publications in bioethics 25 years ago. Since that time, we have in some sense been softened up to the idea of human cloning through movies, cartoons, jokes, and intermittent commentary in the mass media, occasionally serious, more often lighthearted. We have become accustomed to new practices in human reproduction—in vitro fertilization, embryo manipulation, and surrogate pregnancy—and, in animal biotechnology, to transgenic animals and a burgeoning science of genetic engineering.

A High-Stakes Issue

Changes in the broader culture make it now more difficult to express a common, respectful understanding of sexuality, procreation, nascent life, and the meaning of motherhood, fatherhood, and the links between the generations. In a world whose once-given natural boundaries are blurred by technological change and whose moral boundaries are seemingly up for grabs, it is, I believe, much more difficult than it once was to make persuasive the still compelling case against human cloning. . . .

Excerpted with permission from testimony given by Leon R. Kass before the National Bioethics Advisory Commission, March 14, 1997, Washington, D.C. Testimony available at www.texasrighttolife.com/cloning/abacreport_04.html.

Therefore, the first thing of which I want to persuade you is not to be complacent about what is here at issue. Human cloning, though in some respects continuous with previous reproductive technologies, also represents something radically new, both in itself and in its easily foreseeable consequences. The stakes here are very high indeed. Let me exaggerate, but in the direction of the truth: You have been asked to give advice on nothing less than whether human procreation is going to remain human, whether children are going to be made rather than begotten, and whether it is a good thing, humanly speaking, to say yes to the road which leads (at best) to the dehumanized rationality of [Aldous Huxley's dystopian novel] *Brave New World.* If I could persuade you of nothing else, it would be this: What we have here is not business as usual, to be fretted about for a while but finally to be given our seal of approval, not least because it appears to be inevitable. Rise to the occasion, address the subject in all its profundity, and advise as if the future of our humanity may hang in the balance.

> *"Almost no one sees any compelling reason for human cloning; almost everyone anticipates its possible misuses and abuses."*

The Revolting Prospect of Human Cloning

"Offensive." "Grotesque." "Revolting." "Repugnant." "Repulsive." These are the words most commonly heard these days regarding the prospect of human cloning. Such reactions one hears both from the man or woman in the street and from the intellectuals, from believers and atheists, from humanists and scientists. Even [the cloned sheep] Dolly's creator, Dr. [Ian] Wilmot, has said he "would find it offensive" to clone a human being. People are repelled by many aspects of human cloning: The prospect of mass production of human beings, with large clones of look-alikes, compromised in their individuality; the idea of father-son or mother-daughter twins; the bizarre prospects of a woman giving birth to a genetic copy of herself, her spouse, or even her deceased father or mother; the creation of embryonic genetic duplicates of oneself, to be frozen away in case of later need for homologous organ transplantation; the narcissism of those who would clone themselves; the arrogance of others who think they know who deserves to be cloned or which genotype any child-to-be should be thrilled to receive; the Frankensteinian hubris to create human life and increasingly to control its destiny; man playing at being God. Almost no one sees any compelling reason for human cloning; almost everyone anticipates its possible misuses and abuses. Many feel oppressed by the sense that there is nothing we can do to prevent it from happening. This makes the prospect all the more revolting.

Revulsion is surely not an argument, and some of yesterday's repugnances are today calmly accepted. But in crucial cases, repugnance is often the emotional bearer of deep wisdom, beyond reason's power fully to articulate it. Can anyone really give an argument fully adequate to the horror which is father-daughter incest (even with consent) or having sex with animals or eating human flesh, or even just raping or murdering another human being? Would anyone's failure to give full rational justification for his revulsion at these practices make that revulsion ethically suspect? Not at all. In my view, our repugnance at human cloning belongs in this category.

We are repelled by the prospect of cloning human beings not because of the strangeness or novelty of the undertaking, but because we intuit and feel, immediately and without argument, the violation of things we rightfully hold dear. I doubt very much whether I can give the proper rational voice to this horror, but in the remarks that follow I will try. But please consider seriously that this may be one of those instances about which the heart has its reasons that reason cannot adequately know.

Four Primary Objections

I will raise four kinds of objections: the ethics of experimentation; identity and individuality; fabrication and manufacture; despotism and the violation of what it means to have children.

First, any attempt to clone a human being would constitute an unethical experiment upon the resulting child-to-be. As the animal experiments indicate, there is grave risk of mishaps and deformities. Moreover, one cannot presume a future cloned child's consent to be a clone, even a healthy one. Thus, we cannot ethically get to know even whether or not human cloning is feasible.

I understand, of course, the philosophical difficulty of trying to compare life with defects against non-existence. But common sense tells us that it is irrelevant. It is surely true

> *"Any attempt to clone a human being would constitute an unethical experiment upon the resulting child-to-be."*

that people can harm and even maim children in the very act of conceiving them, say, by paternal transmission of the HIV virus or maternal transmission of heroin dependence. To do so intentionally, or even negligently, is inexcusable and clearly unethical.

Second, cloning creates serious issues of identity and individuality. The cloned person may experience concerns about his distinctive identity not only because he will be in genotype and appearance identical to another human being, but, in this case, it will be to a twin who might be his "father" or "mother"—if one can still call them that. What would be the psychic burdens of being the "child" or "parent" of your twin? Moreover, the cloned individual will be saddled with a genotype that has already lived. He will not be fully a surprise to the world: People are likely always to compare his performances in life with that of his alter ego. True, his nurture and circumstance in life will be different; genotype is not exactly destiny. But one must also expect parental and other efforts to shape this new life after the original or at least to view the child with the original version firmly in mind. For why else did they clone from the star basketball player, mathematician, and beauty queen—or even dear old Dad—in the first place?

Genetic distinctiveness not only symbolizes the uniqueness of each human life and the independence of its parents that each human child rightfully attains. It can also be an important support for living a worthy and dignified life. Such arguments apply with great force to any large-scale replication of human individuals. But they are, in my view, sufficient to rebut even the first attempts to clone a human being. One must never forget that these are human beings upon whom our eugenic or merely playful fantasies are to be enacted.

Manufacturing Humans

Third, human cloning would represent a giant step toward turning begetting into making, procreation into manufacture (literally, something "handmade"), a process already begun with in vitro fertilization and genetic testing of embryos. With cloning, not only is the process in hand, but the total genetic blueprint of the cloned individual is selected and determined by the human artisans.

To be sure, subsequent development is still according to natural processes; and the resulting children will still be recognizably human. But we here would be taking a major step into making man himself simply another one of the manmade things. Human nature becomes merely the last part of nature to succumb to the technological project, which turns all of nature into raw material at human disposal, to be homogenized by our rationalized technique according to the subjective prejudices of the day.

How does begetting differ from making? In natural procreation, we two human beings come together, complementarily male and female, to give existence to another being who is formed, exactly as we were, by what we are—living, hence perishable, hence aspiringly erotic human beings. But in clonal reproduction, and in the more advanced forms of manufacture to which it leads, we give existence to a being not by what we are but by what we intend and design. As with any product of our making, no matter how excellent, the artificer stands above it, not as an equal but as a superior, transcending it by his will and creative prowess. Scientists who clone animals make it perfectly clear that they are engaged in instrumental making; the animals are, from the start, designed as means to serve rational human purpose. In human cloning, scientists and prospective "parents" would be adopting the same technocratic mentality to human children: human children would be their artifacts. Such an arrangement is profoundly dehumanizing, no matter how good the product. Mass-scale cloning of the same individual makes the point vividly; but the violation of human equality, freedom, and

> *"Cloning creates serious issues of identity and individuality."*

91

dignity are present even in a single planned clone.

Finally, and perhaps most important, the practice of human cloning by nu-clear transfer—like other anticipated forms of genetic engineering of the next generation—would enshrine and aggravate a profound and mischief-making misunderstanding of the meaning of having children and of the parent-child re-lationship. When a couple now chooses to procreate, the partners are saying yes to the emergence of new life in its novelty, are saying yes not only to having a child but also, tacitly, to having whatever child this child turns out to be. Whether we know it or not, we are thereby also saying yes to our own finitude and mortality, to the necessity of our replacement and the limits of our control. In this ubiquitous way of nature, to say yes to the future by procreating means precisely that we are relinquishing our grip, even as we thereby take up our own share in what we hope will be the immortality of human life and the human species. This means that our children are not our children: They are not our property, they are not our possessions. Neither are they supposed to live our lives for us, or anyone's else's life but their own. To be sure, we seek to guide them on their way, imparting to them not just life but nurture, love, and a way

> **"The violation of human equality, freedom, and dignity are present even in a single planned clone."**

of life; to be sure, they bear our hopes that they will surpass us in goodness and happiness, enabling us in small measure to transcend our own limitations. But their genetic distinctiveness and independence is the natural foreshadowing of the deep truth that they have their own and never-before-enacted life to live. Though sprung from a past, they take an uncharted course into the future.

Much mischief is already done by parents who try to live vicariously through their children; children are sometimes compelled to fulfill the broken dreams of unhappy parents; John Doe Jr. or the III is under the burden of having to live up to his forebear's name. But in cloning, such overbearing parents take at the start a decisive step which contradicts the entire meaning of the open and forward-looking nature of parent-child relations. The child is given a genotype that has already lived, with full expectation that this blueprint of a past life ought to be controlling of the life that is to come. Cloning is inherently despotic, for it seeks to make one's children or someone else's children after one's own image (or an image of one's choosing) and their future according to one's will. In some cases, the despotism may be mild and benevolent, in others, mischievous and downright tyrannical. But despotism—the control of another through one's will—it will unavoidably be.

Unethical and Dangerous

What, then, should we do? We should declare human cloning deeply unethi-cal in itself and dangerous in its likely consequences. In so doing, we shall have the backing of the overwhelming majority not only of our fellow Americans, but of the human race, including, I believe, most practicing scientists. Next, we should do all that we can to prevent human cloning from happening, by an international legal ban if possible, by a unilateral national ban at a minimum. Scientists can, of course, secretly undertake to violate such a law, but they will at least be deterred by not being able to stand up proudly to claim the credit for their technological bravado and success. Such a ban on human cloning will not harm the progress of basic genetic science and technology; on the contrary, it will reassure the public that scientists are happy to proceed without violating the deep ethical norms and intuitions of the human community.

> *"Cloning is inherently despotic, for it seeks to make one's children . . . after one's own image."*

The President has given this Commission a glorious opportunity. In a truly unprecedented way, you can strike a blow for the human control of the technological project, for wisdom, prudence, and human dignity. The prospect of human cloning, so repulsive to contemplate, in fact provides the occasion as well as the urgent necessity of deciding whether we shall be slaves of unregulated progress, and ultimately its artifacts, or whether we shall remain free human beings who guide our technique toward the enhancement of human dignity.

Human Stem Cell Research Is Unethical

by The Center for Bioethics and Human Dignity

About the author: *The Center for Bioethics and Human Dignity, located in Bannockburn, Illinois, studies and addresses contemporary bioethical challenges facing modern society.*

Recent scientific advances in human stem cell research have brought into fresh focus the dignity and status of the human embryo. These advances have prompted a decision by the Department of Health and Human Services (HHS) and the National Institutes of Health (NIH) to fund stem cell research which is dependent upon the destruction of human embryos. Moreover, the National Bioethics Advisory Commission (NBAC) is calling for a modification of the current ban against federally funded human embryo research in order to permit direct federal funding for the destructive harvesting of stem cells from human embryos. These developments require that the legal, ethical, and scientific issues associated with this research be critically addressed and articulated. Our careful consideration of these issues leads to the conclusion that human stem cell research requiring the destruction of human embryos is objectionable on legal, ethical, and scientific grounds. Moreover, destruction of human embryonic life is unnecessary for medical progress, as alternative methods of obtaining human stem cells and of repairing and regenerating human tissue exist and continue to be developed.

Stem Cell Research Violates Existing Laws

In November 1998, two independent teams of U.S. scientists reported that they had succeeded in isolating and culturing stem cells obtained from human embryos and fetuses. Stem cells are the cells from which all 210 different kinds of tissue in the human body originate. Because many diseases result from the death or dysfunction of a single cell type, scientists believe that the introduction of healthy cells of this type into a patient may restore lost or compromised function. Now that human embryonic stem cells can be isolated and multiplied

Reprinted from "On Human Embryos and Stem Cell Research: An Appeal for Legally and Ethically Responsible Science and Public Policy," by The Center for Bioethics and Human Dignity. Reprinted with permission.

in the laboratory, some scientists believe that treatments for a variety of diseases—such as diabetes, heart disease, Alzheimer's, and Parkinson's—may be within reach. While we in no way dispute the fact that the ability to treat or heal suffering persons is a great good, we also recognize that not all methods of achieving a desired good are morally or legally justifiable. If this were not so, the medically accepted and legally required practices of informed consent and of seeking to do no harm to the patient could be ignored whenever some "greater good" seems achievable.

One of the great hallmarks of American law has been its solicitous protection of the lives of individuals, especially the vulnerable. Our nation's traditional protection of human life and human rights derives from an affirmation of the essential dignity of

> *"Human stem cell research requiring the destruction of human embryos is objectionable on legal, ethical, and scientific grounds."*

every human being. Likewise, the international structure of human rights law—one of the great achievements of the modern world—is founded on the conviction that when the dignity of one human being is assaulted, all of us are threatened. The duty to protect human life is specifically reflected in the homicide laws of all 50 states. Furthermore, federal law and the laws of many states specifically protect vulnerable human embryos from harmful experimentation. Yet in recently publicized experiments, stem cells have been harvested from human embryos in ways which destroy the embryos.

Despite an existing congressional ban on federally funded human embryo research, the Department of Health and Human Services (HHS) determined on January 15, 1999, that the government may fund human embryonic stem cell research. The stated rationales behind this decision are that stem cells are not embryos (which itself may be a debatable point) and that research using cells obtained by destroying human embryos can be divorced from the destruction itself. However, even NBAC denies this latter claim, as is evident by the following statement in its May 6, 1999, Draft Report on Stem Cell Research:

> Whereas researchers using fetal tissue are not responsible for the death of the fetus, researchers using stem cells derived from embryos will typically be implicated in the destruction of the embryo. This is true whether or not researchers participate in the derivation of embryonic stem cells. As long as embryos are destroyed as part of the research enterprise, researchers using embryonic stem cells (and those who fund them) will be complicit in the death of embryos.

If the flawed rationales of HHS are accepted, federally funded researchers may soon be able to experiment on stem cells obtained by destroying embryonic human beings, so long as the act of destruction does not itself receive federal funds. However, the very language of the existing ban prohibits the use of federal funds to support "research in which a human embryo or embryos are destroyed, discarded, or knowingly subjected to risk of injury or death. . . ." Obviously, Congress' intent here was not merely to prohibit the use of federal funds for embryo destruction, but to prohibit the use of such funds for research dependent in any way upon such destruction. Therefore, the opinion of HHS that human embryonic stem cell research may receive federal funding clearly violates both the language of and intention behind the existing law. Congress and the courts should ensure that the law is properly interpreted and enforced to ban federal funding for research which harms, destroys, or is dependent upon the destruction of human embryos.

It is important to recognize also that research involving human embryos outside the womb—such as embryos produced in the laboratory by in vitro fertilization (IVF) or cloning—has never received federal funding. Initially, this was because a federal regulation of 1975 prevented government funding of IVF experiments unless such experiments were deemed acceptable by an Ethics Advisory Board. Following the failure of the first advisory board to reach a consensus on the matter, no administration chose to appoint a new board. After this regulation was rescinded by Congress in 1993, the Human Embryo Research Panel recommended to the National Institutes of Health (NIH) that certain kinds of harmful nontherapeutic experiments using human embryos receive federal funding. However, these recommendations were rejected in part by President Bill Clinton and then rejected in their entirety by Congress.

> *"Our nation's traditional protection of human life and human rights derives from an affirmation of the essential dignity of every human being."*

Further, it is instructive to note that the existing law which permits researchers to use fetal tissue obtained from elective abortions requires that the abortions are performed for reasons which are entirely unrelated to the research objectives. This law thus prohibits HHS from promoting the destruction of human life in the name of medical progress, yet medical progress is precisely the motivation and justification offered for the destruction of human life that occurs when stem cells are obtained from human embryos.

Well-Established Legal Precedents

Current law against funding research in which human embryos are harmed and destroyed reflects well-established national and international legal and ethical norms against the misuse of any human being for research purposes. Since 1975, those norms have been applied to unborn children at every stage of development in the womb, and since 1995 they have been applied to the human embryo outside the womb as well. The existing law on human embryonic research is a reflection of universally accepted principles governing experiments on human subjects—principles reflected in the Nuremberg Code, the World Medical

Association's Declaration of Helsinki, the United Nations Declaration of Human Rights, and many other statements. Accordingly, members of the human species who cannot give informed consent for research should not be the subjects of an experiment unless they personally may benefit from it or the experiment carries no significant risk of harming them. Only by upholding such research principles do we prevent treating people as things—as mere means to obtaining knowledge or benefits for others.

It may strike some as surprising that legal protection of embryonic human beings can co-exist with the U.S. Supreme Court's 1973 legalization of abortion. However, the Supreme Court has never prevented the government from protecting prenatal life outside the abortion context, and public sentiment also seems even more opposed to government funding of embryo experimentation than to the funding of abortion. The laws of a number of states—including Louisiana, Maine, Massachusetts, Michigan, Minnesota, Pennsylvania, Rhode Island, and Utah—specifically protect embryonic human beings outside the womb. Most of these provisions prohibit experiments on embryos outside the womb. We believe that the above legally acknowledged protections against assaults on human dignity must be extended to all human beings—irrespective of gender, race, religion, health, disability, or age. Consequently, the human embryo must not be subject to willful destruction even if the stated motivation is to help others. Therefore, on existing legal grounds alone, research using stem cells derived from the destruction of early human embryos is proscribed.

Human Embryonic Stem Cell Research Is Unethical

The HHS decision and the recommendations of NBAC to federally fund research involving the destruction of human embryos would be profoundly disturbing even if this research could result in great scientific and medical gain. The prospect of government-sponsored experiments to manipulate and destroy human embryos should make us all lie awake at night. That some individuals would be destroyed in the name of medical science constitutes a threat to us all. Recent statements claiming that human embryonic stem cell research is too promising to be slowed or prohibited underscore the sort of utopianism and hubris that could blind us to the truth of what we are doing and the harm we could cause to ourselves and others. Human embryos are not mere biological tissues or clusters of cells;

> *"Research involving human embryos outside the womb . . . has never received federal funding."*

they are the tiniest of human beings. Thus, we have a moral responsibility not to deliberately harm them.

An international scientific consensus now recognizes that human embryos are biologically human beings beginning at fertilization and acknowledges the physical continuity of human growth and development from the one-cell stage forward. In the 1970s and 1980s, some frog and mouse embryologists referred to the human embryo in its first week or two of development as a "pre-embryo," claiming that it deserved less respect than embryos in later stages of development. However, some embryology textbooks now openly refer to the term "pre-embryo" as a scientifically invalid and "inaccurate" term which has been "discarded" and others which once used the term have quietly dropped it from new editions. Both the Human Embryo Research Panel and the National Bioethics Advisory Commission have also rejected the term, describing the human embryo from its earliest stages as a living organism and a "developing form of human life." The claim that an early human embryo becomes a human being only after 14 days or implantation in the womb is therefore a scientific myth. Finally, the historic and well-respected 1995 Ramsey Colloquium statement on embryo research acknowledges that:

> *"The human embryo must not be subject to willful destruction even if the stated motivation is to help others."*

> The [embryo] is human; it will not articulate itself into some other kind of animal. Any being that is human is a human being. If it is objected that, at five days or fifteen days, the embryo does not look like a human being, it must be pointed out that this is precisely what a human being looks like—and what each of us looked like—at five or fifteen days of development.

Therefore, the term "pre-embryo," and all that it implies, is scientifically invalid.

The last century and a half has been marred by numerous atrocities against vulnerable human beings in the name of progress and medical benefit. In the 19th century, vulnerable human beings were bought and sold in the town square as slaves and bred as though they were animals. In the 20th century, the vulnerable were executed mercilessly and subjected to demeaning experimentation at Dachau and Auschwitz. At mid-century, the vulnerable were subjects of our own government's radiation experiments without their knowledge or consent. Likewise, vulnerable African-Americans in Tuskegee, Alabama, were victimized as subjects of a government-sponsored research project to study the effects of syphilis. Currently, we are witness to the gross abuse of mental patients used as subjects in purely experimental research. These experiments were and are driven by a crass utilitarian ethos which results in the creation of a "sub-class" of human beings, allowing the rights of the few to be sacrificed for the sake of potential benefit to the many. These unspeakably cruel and inherently wrong acts against human beings have resulted in the enactment of laws and policies which require the protection of human rights and liberties, including the right to be protected from the tyranny of the quest for scientific progress. The painful lessons of the past should have taught us that human beings must not be conscripted for research without their permission—no matter what the alleged justification—especially when that research means the forfeiture of their health or lives. Even if an individual's death is believed to be otherwise imminent, we still do not have a license to engage in lethal experimentation—just as we may not experiment on death row prisoners or harvest their organs without their consent.

We are aware that a number of Nobel scientists endorse human embryonic stem cell research on the basis that it may offer a great good to those who are suffering. While we acknowledge that the desire to heal people is certainly a laudable goal and understand that many have invested their lives in realizing this goal, we also recognize that we are simply not free to pursue good ends via unethical means. Of all human beings, embryos are the most defenseless against abuse. A policy promoting the use and destruction of human embryos would repeat the failures of the past. The intentional destruction of some human beings for the alleged good of other human beings is wrong. Therefore, on ethical grounds alone, research using stem cells obtained by destroying human embryos is ethically proscribed.

Scientifically Questionable

Integral to the decision to use federal funds for research on human embryonic stem cells is the distinction between stem cells and embryos. HHS has stated that federal funds may be used to support human embryonic stem cell research because stem cells are not embryos. A statement issued by the Office of the General Counsel of HHS regarding this decision asserts that "the statutory prohibition on the use of [government] funds . . . for human embryo research would not apply to research utilizing human pluripotent stem cells because such cells are not a human embryo within the statutory definition. [Moreover, because] pluripotent stem cells do not have the capacity to develop into a human being, [they] cannot be considered human embryos consistent with the commonly accepted or scientific understanding of that term."

> *"The prospect of government-sponsored experiments to manipulate and destroy human embryos should make us all lie awake at night."*

It is important to note that the materials used in an experiment, as well as the methods of experimentation, are considered to be part of scientific research. When a scientific study is published, the first part of the article details the methods and materials used to conduct the research. Ethical and scientific evaluation of an experiment takes into account both the methods and materials used in the research process. Therefore, the source of stem cells obtained for research is both a scientifically and ethically relevant consideration.

Research on human embryonic stem cells is objectionable due to the fact that such research necessitates the prior destruction of human embryos; however, the HHS's claim that stem cells are not, and cannot develop into, embryos may itself be subject to dispute. Some evidence suggests that stem cells cultured in the laboratory may have a tendency to recongregate and form an aggregate of cells capable of beginning to develop as an embryo. In 1993, Canadian scientists reported that they successfully produced a live-born mouse from a cluster of mouse stem cells. While it is true that these stem cells had to be wrapped in placenta-like cells in order to implant in a female mouse, it seems that at least some doubt has been cast on the claim that a cluster of stem cells is not embryonic in nature. If embryonic stem cells do indeed possess the ability to form or develop as a human embryo (without any process of activation which affects the transformation of the cell into a human embryo), research on such stem cells could itself involve the creation and/or destruction of human life and would thereby certainly fall under the existing ban on federally funded embryo research. It would be irresponsible for the HHS to conduct and condone human embryonic stem cell research without first discerning the status of these cells. Their use in any research in which they could be converted into human embryos should likewise be banned.

Alternative Methods

While proponents of human embryonic stem cell research lobby aggressively for government funding of research requiring the destruction of human embryos, alternative methods for repairing and regenerating human tissue render such an approach unnecessary for medical progress.

For instance, a promising source of more mature stem cells for the treatment of disease is hematopoietic (blood cell-producing) stem cells from bone marrow or even from the placenta or umbilical cord blood in live births. These cells are already widely used in cancer treatment and in research on treating leukemia and other diseases. Recent experiments have indicated that their versatility is even greater than once thought. For example, given the right environment, bone marrow cells can be used to regenerate muscle tissue, opening up a whole new avenue of potential therapies for muscular dystrophies. In April 1999, new advances were announced in isolating mesenchymal [undifferentiated mesodermal] cells from bone marrow and directing them to form fat, cartilage, and bone tissue. Experts in stem cell research believe that these cells may allow for tissue replacement in patients suffering from cancer, osteoporosis, dental disease, or injury.

"Human beings must not be conscripted for research without their permission— no matter what the alleged justification."

An enormously promising new source of more mature stem cells is fetal bone marrow, a source which is many times more effective than adult bone marrow and umbilical cord blood. It appears that fetal bone marrow cells do not provoke immune reactions to the same degree as adult or even newborn infant cells. This is true whether the unborn child is the donor or the recipient—that is, fetal cells can be used to treat adults, or adult bone marrow cells can be used to treat a child in the womb without the usual risk of harmful immune reactions. Such cells would not need to be derived from fetuses who were intentionally aborted, but could instead be obtained from spontaneously aborted fetuses or stillborn infants.

In 1999, unprecedented advances were also made in isolating and culturing neural stem cells from living human nerve tissue and even from adult cadavers. Such advances render it quite possible that treatment of neural diseases such as Parkinson's and Alzheimer's, as well as spinal cord injuries, will not depend upon destructive embryo research.

> *"The use of [adult stem] cells would not be subject to the ethical and legal objections raised by the use of human embryonic stem cells."*

Earlier claims that embryonic stem cells are uniquely capable of "self-renewal" and indefinite growth can also now be seen as premature. For example, scientists have isolated an enzyme, telomerase, which may allow human tissues to grow almost indefinitely. Although this enzyme has been linked to the development of cancer, researchers have been able to use it in a controlled way to "immortalize" useful tissue without producing cancerous growths or other harmful side effects. Thus, cultures of non-embryonic stem cells may be induced to grow and develop almost indefinitely for clinical use.

Research into the Use of Adult Stem Cells

One of the most exciting new advances in stem cell research is the January 1999 announcement that Canadian and Italian researchers succeeded in producing new blood cells from neural stem cells taken from an adult mouse. Until recently, it was believed that adult stem cells were capable of producing only a particular type of cell: for example, a neural stem cell could develop only into cells belonging to the nervous system. Researchers believed that only embryonic stem cells retained the capacity to form all kinds of tissue in the human body. However, if stem cells taken from adult patients can produce cells and tissues capable of functioning within entirely different systems, new brain tissue needed to treat a patient with Parkinson's disease, for example, might be generated from blood stem cells derived from the patient's bone marrow. Conversely, neural stem cells might be used to produce needed blood and bone marrow. Use of a patient's own stem cells would circumvent one of the major obstacles posed by the use of embryonic stem cells—namely, the danger that tissue taken from another individual would be rejected when transplanted into a patient. Thus, in commenting on this finding, the *British Medical Journal* remarked on January 30, 1999, that the use of embryonic stem cells "may soon be eclipsed by the more readily available and less controversial adult stem cells." Given that the function of the adult stem cells was converted without the cells first having to pass through an embryonic stage, the use of such cells would not be subject to the ethical and legal objections raised by the use of human embryonic stem cells. The Director of the NIH has pointed out that evidence that adult stem cells can take on different functions has emerged only from studies on mice. However, his own claim that human embryonic stem cell research can produce treatments for diabetes and other diseases is also based solely on experimental success in mice.

One approach to tissue regeneration that does not rely on stem cells at all, but on somatic cell gene therapy, is already in use as an experimental treatment. A gene that controls production of growth factors can be injected directly into a patient's own cells, with the result that new blood vessels will develop. In early trials, this type of therapy saved the legs of patients who would have otherwise undergone amputation. It was reported in January 1999 that the technique has generated new blood vessels in the human heart and improved the condition of 19 out of 20 patients with blocked cardiac blood vessels. Such growth factors are now being explored as a means for growing new organs and tissues of many kinds.

The above recent advances suggest that it is not even necessary to obtain stem cells by destroying human embryos in order to treat disease. A growing number of researchers believe that adult stem cells may soon be used to develop treatments for afflictions such as cancer, immune disorders, orthopedic injuries, congestive heart failure, and degenerative diseases. Such researchers are working to further research on adult, rather than embryonic, stem cells. In light of these promising new scientific advances, we urge Congress to provide federal funding for the development of methods to repair and regenerate human tissue which do not require the destruction of embryonic human life. However, even if such methods do not prove to be as valuable in treating disease as are human embryonic stem cells, use of the latter in the name of medical progress is still neither legally nor ethically justifiable for the reasons stated in this document.

Concluding Recommendations

We believe that an examination of the legal, ethical, and scientific issues associated with human embryonic stem cell research leads to the conclusion that the use of federal funds to support any such research that necessitates the destruction of human embryos is, and should remain, prohibited by law. Therefore, we call on Congress to (1) maintain the existing ban against harmful federally funded human embryo research and make explicit its application to stem cell research requiring the destruction of human embryos and (2) provide federal funding for the development of alternative treatments which do not require the destruction of human embryonic life. If anything is to be gained from the cruel atrocities committed against human beings in the last century and a half, it is the lesson that the utilitarian devaluation of one group of human beings for the alleged benefit of others is a price we simply cannot afford to pay.

Allowing the Sale of Human Organs Would Not Be Ethical

by Atul Gawande

About the author: *Physician Atul Gawande writes a regular column on science and policy for* Slate, *an on-line magazine.*

Letting people peddle their kidneys might save lives, but the ethical price is too high.

Some people clearly are itching to do it. Consider this classified ad from Ruth Sparrow, a 55-year-old woman who was $20,000 short for a needed gallbladder operation, which ran in the May 17, 1997, *St. Petersburg Times* under "medical supplies": "KIDNEY—Runs good, Taking offers. $30,000/obo."

Someone must have called the newspaper, because it pulled the ad after three days, noting that organ selling is against federal law. That didn't stop John Curtis, though. The 63-year-old immigrant from England managed to slip this ad into the same newspaper on May 10, 1998: "BRITISH MADE Kidney shaped item; will swap for 45' motor/sailboat." When it came out that he was selling one of his kidneys, the newspaper pulled his ad, too.

The Argument for Allowing Organ Selling

Awful, right? Not at all, some say. Organ selling is gaining a respectable fan club. Recently, the Cato Institute posted an article on its Web site backing organ markets, and former Delaware Gov. Pete du Pont, policy chairman of the National Center for Policy Analysis, has endorsed the idea. Its most sophisticated defense, however, comes from University of Chicago law Professor Richard Epstein.

Epstein is pursuing an honorable but difficult mission. He wants to alleviate the enormous shortage of organs for transplantation. He also wants to bring libertarianism into medicine, an arena in which few ideologues survive. In his book *Mortal Peril* and a *Wall Street Journal* op-ed, he stakes a simple claim:

Even in health care, people should be allowed to do what they wish with their own bodies (as long as they don't hurt anyone else). And that includes selling their body parts. It's not just because he believes people have the right. It's because he thinks giving people that freedom will save lives.

It's harder to refute Epstein than you might think. He is probably right about saving lives. The transplant waiting list currently includes 55,560

> *"What about the risk that some people will be coerced or will act impulsively?"*

patients, and about four thousand of them will die waiting. Healthy people could conceivably sell their eyes, some skin, a few bones, a kidney, a portion of their liver, and even a lung and still survive. If Epstein's organ market opened for business, patients with the resources would certainly bid up prices enough to attract sellers. Perhaps, as he says, charity will even raise money for patients who can't pay the going rate. ("If you could spare just a couple of dollars, ma'am, we'll have enough to buy someone a beautiful cornea.")

Epstein has a ready response for the arguments. Won't organ selling draw down-and-outs with lower quality organs? So what, he says. The market will reduce the price for their organs, testing will weed out unacceptable risks, and the risks will outweigh the lives saved anyway. What about the risk that some people will be coerced or will act impulsively? He says that we can do careful screening and require waiting periods. Aren't people who sell their organs out of desperate financial need acting involuntarily? No more so than when they stoop to cleaning bathrooms for minimum wage, he says. You might reply that this isn't just cleaning out toilet bowls. But, he says, if you're really worried about exploiting the poor, then we can require a minimum income for anyone who sells their organs.

Unreliable Reasoning

Well, I am no philosopher, and I remain unencumbered by legal training, but I still believe the whole idea is warped. My opposition stems from exposure to ordinary people as they make decisions about whether to undergo surgery, to take their medicines, and so on. Libertarians have great faith that people nearly always make rational choices and that having more choices can't be bad. But any doctor can tell you that's not true. In medicine, you come to recognize how unreliable the faculty of reasoning is and how susceptible it is to subtle forms of exploitation.

Consider a common decision faced by patients with asymptomatic carotid stenosis, a blockage of the carotid artery. These patients have about an 11 percent chance of a stroke or death in five years. Surgery to remove the blockage carries a 2 percent risk of causing immediate stroke or death, but the five-year risk is just 5 percent. Patients must decide whether the upfront risk of surgery is worth cutting their overall risk of having a stroke in half. It's not an easy task.

Each individual must define what's most important in his or her life, then calculate the best course to meet these goals. I can tell you that a lot of people fail to reason through the options very well. Even when they understand their goals clearly, they often pick a choice that runs against their aims. In academician's terms, they fail to maximize their self-interest.

Studies have shown that the brain has systematic faults in reasoning, especially when processing risk information like this. For example, the order in which a doctor presents options can easily sway people. Also, saying people are fine 98 percent of the time after surgery can lead patients one way, while saying people experience strokes 2 percent of the time can lead them in the other direction. Yet there is no right way to frame the options. Another quirk, as gamblers and con artists know all too well, is that the brain is not good at weighing small chances of big gains (or losses) against large chances of small losses (or gains).

When an organ seller is trying to decide whether the terrible dangers from kidney removal or the certain loss of sight from surrendering an eye is worth a sudden cash infusion, his effort to identify his best interest will be confused by how the question is framed, by difficulties sorting out the statistical risks, by the vision of all that money, and many other factors. These vulnerabilities are easily exploited. But even when not taken advantage of, plenty of people get serious decisions wrong—enough that we should question libertarian beliefs that people should do what they want and live with the consequences.

The Need to Outlaw Terrible Options

Some options are so terrible and irrevocable, so unlikely to be in a person's self-interest, and so open to exploitation and flawed decision-making that society outlaws them. In human experimentation, for example, researchers cannot pay volunteers so much that the poor could be exploited. Rules limit how much blood you can donate or sell at one sitting. And while we allow people to give a kidney to their child, we do not allow them to donate their heart. Likewise, hawking an organ would be right for so few, if any, that permitting the option makes no sense at all.

Isn't this paternalism? Yes. Even Epstein seems to recognize we need some when he accepts laws stopping people from selling themselves into

> *"Hawking an organ would be right for so few, if any."*

slavery or selling a vital organ such as their heart. People will argue about where to draw the line. Some think seat belt laws, for example, go too far. But few would discard laws against organ selling.

I know that I could find myself on that transplant waiting list someday. But I'll take my chances. It's certainly better than living in a society that allows money to entice people to convert their own health into a commodity. People can be weak, and money is all too often the way to their heart.

Organ Donation from Anencephalic Infants Is Unethical

by Paul C. Fox

About the author: *Paul C. Fox is a medical doctor in Farmington, Pennsylvania.*

Not so many years ago death was a simple enough concept. If a person's heart ceased to beat for any great length of time he was dead, and that was that. Then along came medical technology, and suddenly what had been simple became complicated. Now a person's heart can be stopped completely for hours, and yet, thanks to the heart-lung machine, that person's brain will survive undamaged. The person is dead by the old definition, yet obviously not really dead. On the other hand—again thanks to medical technology—a person's brain can be irreparably destroyed, even though the heart may be kept beating for many hours. The person is still alive by the old definition, yet most of us instinctively feel that he is somehow not really living.

When Does Death Occur?

The altered perception of what constitutes life and death underlies the ethical dilemmas surrounding organ transplantation today. Of course, there is no controversy if, for example, a living person voluntarily donates a kidney to a relative who needs one. No one has to die in order for the transplant to be performed. This is not the case, however, with transplantations of such vital organs as the heart, the lungs, and the liver, where the donor must necessarily be dead before the transplantation can take place. Yet since, even with the best available medical technology, the organs deteriorate fairly rapidly, they must be "harvested" (in the macabre terminology of transplantation) when the donor is— you'll pardon the expression—"freshly dead." In other words, there is a considerable urgency about removing the donor's organs as soon as possible after his death. At the same time, there is also an overwhelming need to prevent "prema-

Reprinted from "Babies and Body Parts," by Paul C. Fox, *First Things*, December 1994. Reprinted with permission from *First Things*. Article available at www.firstthings.com/ftissues/ft9412/opinion.html.

ture removal," i.e., removing the vital organs of a person who is not yet dead.

To deal with these problems, the medical community has developed strict criteria for defining what is called "brain death." These criteria are extremely detailed and, until now, very much biased toward presuming that life continues: there is virtually no possibility that a person who is actually still living will be proclaimed dead. For example, someone who has been comatose for years, and whose responsiveness is limited to a few primitive reflexes, will still not qualify as "brain dead" by these criteria. Neither will an anencephalic baby; that is, a baby born with no cerebral cortex but with enough brain matter to permit primitive reflexes. And that brings us to the latest development in the ethics of transplantation.

> *"An anencephalic baby is still a* **baby** *after all."*

Consider the following. Of all the children whose lives could be saved by an organ transplant, half die because of a shortage of donated organs. On the other hand, anencephalic babies, who are born with almost no brain but are otherwise physically normal, can only survive a few days after birth. On the surface, it seems like an almost perfect match: the organs of a baby who cannot live can be used to rescue another child who must otherwise die. That, at least, is how it looked to physicians at Loma Linda University in 1987, when they set up a special program designed to salvage the organs of anencephalic babies for transplantation. However, in eight months of operation the program failed to salvage even one viable organ. Why? Simply because these babies were not "brain dead" at birth: impaired as they were, they retained enough brain function to fail the criteria for death. By the time these babies finally did die, their organs had suffered severe damage and were no longer usable.

The physicians and nurses at Loma Linda accepted their defeat, some of them with considerable relief. An anencephalic baby is still a *baby* after all, and the act of inflicting intensive care on a dying infant simply in order to be able to harvest its organs after death began to take an emotional toll on the staff.

The "Baby Theresa" Case

There are some, however, who are not so willing to relinquish this potential source of donor organs. In 1992 the Florida State Supreme Court heard the "Baby Theresa" case. In this case the parents, backed by the American Civil Liberties Union (ACLU), requested that their anencephalic baby be declared dead at birth, even though she did not meet the accepted criteria for brain death, so that her heart could be transplanted into another child. One can only guess what the parents' motives and feelings were. Perhaps they were trying to assuage guilt feelings or offer themselves comfort by trying to bring some good out of a tragic situation. Perhaps they were able, by some exercise of self-hypnosis, to avoid realizing what would actually be done to their baby: that she would be taken to an operating room, and there—even though she was able to breathe, kick, and cry—her heart would be removed for use as a "donor organ."

The reasoning of the ACLU in this case was chilling. They noted "the inconsistency of permitting the termination of pregnancies up to the moment of birth" while at the same time "prohibiting the donation of organs just after birth." As they put it, "There is absolutely no morally significant change in the fetus between the moments immediately preceding and following birth." Note that exactly the same argument used by the pro-life movement for years in defending the unborn is now being used by the ACLU to justify infanticide.

It is not hard to see where this reasoning leads. Though the ACLU denies that its position "serves as a springboard to institutional murder," it clearly does just that. The reasoning used to justify declaring anencephalic babies "dead" at birth can be applied with equal logic to any other baby whose deformities might have moved its parents to abort it, had they but known of them. In fact, this reasoning really strips all newborns of any protection. If abortion on demand "up to the very moment of birth" is morally acceptable, as the ACLU asserts, why not infanticide on demand? And why stop at infants? There are millions of retarded children and adults whose lives are below the high standards of the social engineers. Why not declare them dead as well? At a stroke, the organ shortage could be solved.

> *"Even though she was able to breathe, kick, and cry—her heart would be removed for use as a 'donor organ.'"*

Fortunately, the Florida Supreme Court had the uncommon (these days) good sense to reject the ACLU's arguments. Baby Theresa was allowed to live out her short life without being terminated for some "higher good." But it was too much to hope that the notion of harvesting organs from handicapped infants would die with her.

In the summer of 1994, no less an authority than the American Medical Association (AMA) Council on Ethical and Judicial Affairs declared that it is "ethically permissible" for anencephalic infants to be used as donors while still alive. In its opinion, the Council admitted that it is normally preferable for an organ donor to be dead before removing vital organs, but made an exception in the case of anencephalics for two main reasons: first, "because of the great need for children's organs," and second, because anencephalics "have never experienced, and will never experience, consciousness." Or, as one supporter of the decision bluntly put it, "The quality of life for this child is so low it would be ethically justifiable to sacrifice its life by a few days to save the life of another person."

Extending the Reasoning to Others

Such reasoning cannot be confined to the narrow case of anencephalics. Due to improvements in prenatal care the incidence of anencephaly has declined steadily, so that fewer than one hundred babies with anencephaly are likely to be born in the United States each year, and many of them are born with such serious organ defects that they would be excluded as organ donors. Clearly, anencephalics alone would not begin to address the "great need for children's organs" that the Council cited in justifying its decision.

The Council's decision must be seen for what it is—the thin edge of the wedge. Using the dual arguments of "no possibility of consciousness" and "poor quality of life," it will not be difficult to extend the Council's reasoning widely. What about children and adults in a "persistent vegetative state"? If in the judgment of the medical experts such people no longer have the possibility of consciousness, what ethical obstacle remains to removing their vital organs? What about the profoundly retarded who, as all compassionate social planners will agree, have a "low quality of life"? What about a child with third-degree burns over 90 percent of his body? He has no chance of survival, and an obviously low quality of life, yet his heart is beating strongly— a heart that another child could use. Why not end the needless suffering of one child, and give the gift of life to another through one painless and humane operation?

> *"This reasoning really strips all newborns of any protection."*

Unthinkable? Think again. Think first of everything that was unthinkable thirty years ago and is now commonplace: abortion on demand, the growing acceptance of euthanasia, genetic engineering, cloning, and so on. Think of the unthinkable Holocaust. The ideas behind that horror originated not with the Nazis but with the "humane" social scientists of Germany's finest universities. Then think of the combined resources of the AMA and the ACLU turned against the Baby Theresas of our society. We must anticipate the unthinkable, or the unthinkable will become routine.

Chapter 4

How Can Ethical Behavior Be Taught?

Teaching Children Ethical Behavior: An Overview

by Wray Herbert

About the author: *Wray Herbert is a senior writer for* U.S. News & World Report, *a weekly news magazine.*

Only in contemporary America could selecting a family anthology be considered a political act. On one cultural flank is famous Republican moralist William Bennett's bestselling *Book of Virtues,* a hefty collection of tales, fables and poems celebrating universal virtues such as courage, compassion and honesty. Side by side with the Bennett tome in many bookstores is Herbert Kohl and Colin Greer's *A Call to Character,* a similar assemblage of proverbs and stories organized around equally cherished values. No one could blame the casual browser for arbitrarily grabbing one or the other. But it's not a casual choice. These two volumes represent a fundamental and acrimonious division over what critics call the most pressing issue facing our nation today: how we should raise and instruct the next generation of American citizens.

A Fundamental Division over Ethics

The differences between the two volumes of moral instruction aren't even that subtle, once you're familiar with the vocabulary of America's culture war. Both agree on qualities of character like kindness and responsibility. But look deeper: Is unwavering patriotism more desirable than moral reasoning? Does discretion trump courage, or the other way around? Read the *Book of Virtues* to your children and they'll learn about valor from William Tell and Henry V at Agincourt. Read from *A Call to Character* and their moral instructors will be Arnold Lobel's decidedly unheroic but very human Frog and Toad. The former has sections devoted to work, faith and perseverance; the latter, playfulness, balance and adaptability. It's not just semantics or moral hairsplitting. These dueling miscellanies symbolize a much wider struggle for the hearts and minds of America's kids.

Child rearing has always been filled with ambiguities. But while parents once

Excerpted from "The Moral Child," by Wray Herbert, *U.S. News & World Report,* June 3, 1996. Reprinted with permission.

riffled through their Dr. Spock and other how-to manuals for helpful perspectives on toilet training and fussy eaters, today the questions and concerns seem to have moved beyond the scope of child psychology and the familiar hearthside dilemmas. The issue for today's parents is how to raise decent kids in a complex and morally ambiguous world where traditional tethers to church, school and neighborhood are badly frayed. Capturing the heightened concerns of thousands of par-

> *"The issue for today's parents is how to raise decent kids in a complex and morally ambiguous world."*

ents from around the country . . . , one 41-year-old mother observes about raising her teenage daughter: "It's not just dealing with chores and curfews. That stuff's easy. But what do you do when the values you believe in are being challenged every day at the high school, the mall, right around the corner in your own neighborhood?"

It's a sign of how high the stakes have risen that both first lady Hillary Rodham Clinton and former Vice President Dan Quayle have weighed in with books on proper moral child rearing. Both are motivated by fear that the moral confusion of today's youth could be deleterious to our democracy, which draws its sustenance and vitality from new generations of competent and responsible citizens. There's a sense of desperation in current writing about moral parenting, a sense that, as one psychologist puts it, improper child rearing has become a "public health problem" requiring urgent attention. Some lawmakers and public officials are even agitating for creation of a national public policy on the cultivation of private character.

The perceived threat to the commonweal varies, of course, depending on one's political perspective. Critics on the right view moral relativity and indulgent parenting as the cause of today's moral confusion and call for the rediscovery of firmness, regimentation, deference and piety to counter our culture's decline. Those on the left are alarmed at what they see as a wave of simplistic nostalgia gaining force in the country: In their view, it is a bullying reformation designed to mold moral automatons incapable of genuine judgment or citizenship.

The split is political, not scientific. Psychological understanding of moral development is actually quite sophisticated and consistent. For example, decades of research leave little doubt that empathy—the ability to assume another's point of view—develops naturally in the first years of life. Parents, of course, know this just from casual observation. Even infants show unmistakable signs of distress when another child is hurt or upset, and rudimentary forms of sympathy and helping—offering a toy to a distraught sibling, for example—can be observed in children as young as 1. Most psychologists who study empathy assume that the basic skill is biologically wired, probably created along with the bonds of trust that an infant forms with a caretaker, usually the mother. The task for parents is not so much a matter of teaching empathy as not quashing its natural flowering.

Building Blocks

Empathy is the bedrock of human morality, the emotional skill required for the emergence of all other moral emotions—shame, guilt, pride and so forth. Almost every form of moral behavior imaginable—from doing chores responsibly to sacrificing one's life for a cause—is inconceivable without it. Yet empathy is not enough. A second crucial building block of morality is self-discipline, and psychologists have some solid evidence about how this moral "skill" is nurtured.

Most parents tend to adopt one of three general "styles" of interacting with their kids, each style a different combination of three basic factors: acceptance and warmth (vs. rejection), firmness (vs. leniency) and respect for autonomy (vs. control). How parents combine these traits sends very different messages to their children, which over time are "internalized" in such character traits as self-esteem, self-control, social competence and responsibility—or, of course, in the absence of those traits.

There is little doubt about what works and what doesn't. In fact, says Temple University child psychologist Laurence Steinberg, author of a new study called *Beyond the Classroom,* extensive research over many years shows that parents who are more accepting and warm, firmer about rules and discipline and more supportive of their child's individuality produce healthier kids: "No research has ever suggested that children fare better when their parents are aloof than when they are accepting, when their parents are lenient rather than firm, or when their parents are psychologically controlling, rather than supportive of their psychological autonomy."

Psychologists call this ideal parenting style "authoritative" parenting, a middle ground between "autocratic" and "permissive" parenting, both of which tend to produce untoward consequences for children in terms of both competence and integrity. The need to control children appears to be especially damaging to self-discipline. "Parents who are high in control," Steinberg says, "tend to value obedience over independence. They are likely to tell their children that young people should not question adults, that their opinions count less because they are children, and so on. Expressions of individuality are frowned upon in these families and equated with signs of disrespect."

> *"Critics on the right view moral relativity and indulgent parenting as the cause of today's moral confusion and call for the rediscovery of firmness [and] regimentation."*

The best con men, of course, combine self-discipline with a keen ability to read others' thoughts and feelings. Morality requires more—specifically, the ability to think about such things as justice and fairness and ultimately to act on those thoughts. According to the late psychologist Lawrence Kohlberg of Harvard University, people pass through six fairly inflexible "stages" of moral reasoning, beginning with a childlike calculation of self-interest and ending with the embodiment of abstract principles of justice. The ability to think logically about right and wrong, Kohlberg believed, was essential to the development of complete moral beings: Moral habits and emotions alone, he argued, were inadequate for dealing with novel moral dilemmas or when weighing one value against another, as people often must do in real life.

Moral Identity

Psychologists emphasize the importance of young children's "internalizing" values, that is, absorbing standards that are then applied in different times, places or situations. In a study called *Learning to Care,* Princeton sociologist Robert Wuthnow argues that teenagers basically need to go through a second experience of internalization if they are to become caring adults. Just as young children absorb and integrate a rudimentary understanding of kindness and caring from watching adult models, adolescents need to witness a more nuanced form of caring, to absorb "stories" of adult generosity and self-sacrifice. That way, they see that involvement is a real possibility in a world where so much caring has been institutionalized.

> *"Critics [on the left] charge that . . . preoccupation with drill and habit suggests a dark and cynical view of human nature."*

Similarly, a recent study suggests that people who have chosen lives of lifelong, passionate commitment have had more opportunities than most people to develop appropriate trust, courage and responsible imagination. There is no such thing as a "Gandhi pill," Lesley College Prof. Laurent Parks Daloz and his colleagues write in the book *Common Fire,* but there are commonly shared experiences: a parent committed to a cause, service opportunities during adolescence, cross-cultural experiences, a rich mentoring experience in young adulthood. Often, the authors conclude, the committed differ from the rest of us only by having more of these experiences, and deeper ones.

Force of Habit

Of course, cultural battles rarely reflect the complexity of human behavior, and the current debate about proper moral child rearing has a black-and-white quality. As Bennett writes in his introduction to the *Book of Virtues,* moral education involves "explicit instruction, exhortation, and training. Moral education *must* provide training in good habits." But critics charge that such preoccupation with drill and habit suggests a dark and cynical view of human nature as a bundle of unsavory instincts that need constant squelching and reining in. In theology, it's called original sin; in psychological terms, it's a "behaviorist" approach, conditioning responses—or habits—which eventually become automatic and no longer require the weighing of moral options. The opposing philosophy—drawing from the romanticism of Jean Jacques Rousseau, psychology's "human potential" movement and the "constructivist" movement in education—emphasizes the child's natural empathy and untapped potential for reasoning.

> *"Hundreds of schools and districts have adopted strategies for addressing morals and civic virtue."*

The Clinton and Quayle volumes show how simplistic psychology can make for unsophisticated public philosophy. There's no question that the first lady's *It Takes a Village* is informed by an overriding respect for children as essentially competent beings who need nurturance to blossom. But critics see Clinton's optimism as dewy eyed and unrealistic, too much akin to the self-esteem movement and a "child centered" parenting style that allows kids to become morally soft. Quayle's *The American Family,* by contrast, endorses control and punishment as "a way to shape behavior toward respect and obedience." He notes approvingly that the five healthy families he studied reject the counsel of "prominent child experts," including the well-documented finding that spanking and other forms of physical coercion teach violence rather than values.

Quayle's analysis is only one of many calls to return to a time when children knew their proper place and society was not so disorderly. Perhaps the strongest prescription is *The Perversion of Autonomy* by psychiatrist Willard Gaylin and political theorist Bruce Jennings, both of New York's Hastings Center for bioethics. The book is a gleeful celebration of the value of coercion. In the view of these authors, the manifest vulgarities of liberal society justify and demand a serious rollback of the dubious advances of the civil rights era; for the good of society, it follows, children require early and decisive flattening.

There is little question that the worst of New Age gobbledygook makes the cultural left an easy target for attack. One parent tells the story of when her 6-year-old was caught stealing at school. She met with the teacher, hoping together they could come up with a strategy to make it clear that stealing was unacceptable. But the teacher's response astonished her: "We don't use the word *stealing* here," she said. "We call it *uncooperative behavior.*" Few defend such foolish excesses of the self-esteem movement. But progressives argue they are aberrations used to attack liberal parenting and pedagogy. It's naive to focus on examples of indulgence, they argue, when if anything our culture is a child-hating culture, with family policies to match.

Classroom Politics

This same ideological tug of war can be observed in the nation's schools, specifically in battles over the so-called character education movement. Only a few years old, the movement is fairly diverse, in some schools involving a specific packaged curriculum and reading materials, in others more of a philosophy or administrative style. But the general idea has captured the attention of the White House and Congress, both of which are searching for an appropriate federal role in promoting basic decency. Lawmakers have lent their symbolic support by endorsing "National Character Counts Week." The Department of Education has funded a few pilot programs and will soon fund a few more. And in June 1996, President Bill Clinton addressed a joint White House–congressional conference on character building, the third such meeting sponsored by this administration.

Many states have also created character education requirements, and by conservative estimate, hundreds of schools and districts have adopted strategies for addressing morals and civic virtue. Precisely because of the diversity of philosophies that fall under the rubric "character education," experts say, parents need to be aware of what the term means in their own child's classroom.

For example, some schools have adopted conservative models that tend to emphasize order, discipline and courage—what Boston University educator Kevin Ryan labels the "stern virtues," as opposed to "soft" or easy virtues like compassion and self-esteem. Such programs don't shy away from unfashion-

> *"Some schools have adopted conservative models that tend to emphasize order, discipline and courage."*

able ideas like social control and indoctrination, says University of Illinois sociologist Edward Wynne, a guiding light of this approach and coauthor, with Ryan, of *Reclaiming Our Schools*. Wynne calls for a return to the "great tradition in education," that is, the transmission of "good doctrine" to the next generation. Because of the "human propensity for selfishness," Wynne encourages schools to use elaborate reward systems, including "ribbons, awards and other signs of moral merit." The model also emphasizes group sports and pep rallies as effective ways to elevate school spirit. Variations of this reward-and-discipline model emphasize drilling in a prescribed set of values, often focusing on a "virtue of the month."

Programs based on the stern virtues also tend to emphasize institutional loyalty and submission of the individual to the larger community. Ryan points to Roxbury Latin, a 350-year-old private boys' school in Boston, as an example of this approach. The school subscribes to an unambiguous set of Judeo-Christian values—honesty, courtesy and respect for others, according to the catalog. It attempts to inculcate these values through a classical curriculum, through mandatory, sermonlike "halls" and through formal and casual interactions between teachers (called "masters") and students. No racial, ethnic or religious student organizations are permitted, in order to encourage loyalty to the larger school community. According to Headmaster F. Washington Jarvis, an Episcopal priest, Roxbury Latin's view of human nature is much like the Puritan founders': "mean, nasty, brutish, selfish, and capable of great cruelty and meanness. We have to hold a mirror up to the students and say, 'This is who you are. Stop it.'"

Roxbury Latin teaches kids to rein in their negative impulses not with harsh discipline, however, but with love and security of belonging. Displays of affection are encouraged, according to Jarvis, and kids are disciplined by being made to perform (and report) good deeds—a powerful form of behavior modification. Students are rebuked and criticized when they stray, but criticism is always followed by acts of caring and acceptance. Whenever a student is sent to Jarvis's office for discipline, the headmaster always asks as the boy leaves, "Do I love you?"

Ethical Dilemmas

At the other end of the spectrum are character education programs that emphasize moral reasoning. These, too, vary a great deal, but most are derived at least loosely from the work of Kohlberg and other stage theorists. Strict Kohlbergian programs tend to be highly cognitive, with students reasoning through hypothetical moral dilemmas and often weighing conflicting values in order to arrive at judgments of right and wrong. A classic Kohlbergian dilemma, for example, asks whether it's right for a poor man to steal medicine to save his dying wife. Even young children tend to justify dishonesty in this situation, but only adults do so based on a firmly held principle of what's unchallengeably right. Kohlbergian programs are also much more likely to have kids grapple with controversial social dilemmas, since it's assumed that the same sort of moral logic is necessary for citizens to come to informed decisions on the issues of the day—whether gay lifestyles ought to be tolerated in the U.S. Navy, for example.

Variations in programs on strict moral reasoning are generally based on a kind of "constructivist" model of education, in which kids have to figure out for themselves, based on real experiences, what makes the other person feel better or worse, what rules make sense, who makes decisions. Kids actively struggle with issues and from the inside out "construct" a notion of what kind of moral person they want to be. (Advocates of moral reasoning are quick to distinguish this approach from "values clarification," a 1960s educational fad and a favorite whipping boy of conservative reformers. Values clarification consisted of a variety of exercises aimed at helping kids figure out what was most important to them, regardless of how selfish or cruel those "values" might be. It's rarely practiced today.)

"At the other end of the spectrum are character education programs that emphasize moral reasoning."

The Hudson school system in Massachusetts is a good example of this constructivist approach. The program is specifically designed to enhance the moral skills of empathy and self-discipline. Beginning in kindergarten, students participate in role-playing exercises, a series of readings about ethical dilemmas in history and a variety of community service programs that have every Hudson student, K through 12, actively engaged in helping others and the community. Environmental efforts are a big part of the program: Kindergartners, for instance, just completed a yearlong recycling project. The idea, according to Superintendent Sheldon Berman, is for children to understand altruism both as giving to the needy today and as self-sacrifice for future generations. By contrast, the conservative "Character Education Manifesto" states explicitly: "Character education is *not* about acquiring the right *views*," including "currently accepted attitudes about ecology."

Needless to say, these philosophical extremes look very different in practice. Parents who find one or the other more appealing will almost certainly have different beliefs about human behavior. But the best of such programs, regardless of ruling philosophy, share in one crucial belief: that making decent kids requires constant repetition and amplification of basic moral messages. Both Roxbury Latin and Hudson, for example, fashion themselves as "moral communities," where character education is woven into the basic fabric of the school and reflected in every aspect of the school day.

Community Voices

This idea is consistent with the best of moral development theory. According to Brown University developmental psychologist William Damon, author of *Greater Expectations,* "Real learning is made up of a thousand small experiences in a thousand different relationships, where you see all the facets of courage, caring and respect." Virtue-of-the-week programs will never work, Damon contends, because they lack moral dimension and trivialize moral behavior. Children can handle moral complexity, he says, and sense what's phony. "Kids need a sense of purpose, something to believe in. Morality is not about prohibitions, things to avoid, be afraid of or feel guilty about."

Building this sense of purpose is a task beyond the capacity of most families today. The crucial consistency of a moral message requires that kids hear it not only from their parents but from their neighbors, teachers, coach, the local policeman.

> *"The crucial consistency of a moral message requires that kids hear it not only from their parents but from their neighbors, teachers, coach, the local policeman."*

Unfortunately, Damon says, few do. The culture has become so adversarial that the important figures in a child's life are more apt to be at one another's throats than presenting a unified moral front. Litigiousness has become so widespread that it even has a name, the "parents' rights movement." More than ever before, parents see themselves primarily as advocates for their children's rights, suing schools over every value conflict. In a New York case now making its way through the courts, for example, parents are suing because they object to the school district's community service requirement.

Moral Ecology

The irony of postmodern parenting, writes sociologist David Popenoe in *Seedbeds of Virtue,* is that just when science has produced a reliable body of knowledge about what makes decent kids, the key elements are disintegrating: the two-parent family, the church, the neighborhood school and a safe, nurturing community. Popenoe and others advocate a much broader understanding of what it means to raise a moral child today—what communitarian legal theorist Mary Ann Glendon calls an "ecological approach" to child rearing, which views parents and family as just one of many interconnecting "seedbeds" that can contribute to a child's competency and character.

> *"Just when science has produced a reliable body of knowledge about what makes decent kids, the key elements are disintegrating."*

Hillary Clinton borrowed for her book title the folk wisdom, "It takes a village to raise a child." It's an idea that seems to be resonating across the political spectrum today, even in the midst of rough cultural strife. Damon, for example, ended his book with the inchoate notion of "youth charters," an idea that he says has taken on a life of its own. He has been invited into communities from Texas to New England to help concerned citizens identify shared values and develop plans for modeling and nurturing these values in newly conceived moral communities.

Americans are hungry for this kind of moral coherence, Damon says, and although they need help getting past their paralysis, it's remarkable how quickly they can reach consensus on a vision for their kids and community. He is optimistic about the future: "My great hope is that we can actually rebuild our communities in this country around our kids. That's one great thing about America: people love their kids. They've just lost the art of figuring out how to raise them."

Character Education Programs Teach Students Ethical Behavior

by Sanford N. McDonnell

About the author: *Sanford N. McDonnell is the chairman of the Character Education Partnership, an organization based in Washington, D.C., that encourages schools to stress ethics. He is also chairman emeritus of McDonnell Douglas Corporation, an aerospace company in St. Louis, Missouri.*

In 1748 Baron Charles de Montesquieu published his magnum opus, *The Spirit of Laws,* a work that had a profound effect upon our founding fathers. In it Montesquieu developed the concept of the separation of powers, which formed the basis of our Constitution over two hundred years ago. In his work Montesquieu also explored the relationship which must exist between a people and their governments without which that form of government cannot survive. For example, a dictatorship depends upon fear and when fear disappears the dictatorship is overthrown. A monarchy depends upon the loyalty of the people and dies when loyalty dies. The most desirable form of government is a free republic, obviously; but it is also the most fragile form of government because it depends upon a virtuous people. What did he mean by a "virtuous" people? Virtuous means living by high ethical values. What do we mean by ethics? One of the best definitions was given by Dr. Albert Schweitzer: "In a general sense, ethics is the name that we give to our concern for good behavior. We feel an obligation to consider not only our own personal well-being but also that of others and of human society as a whole." Montesquieu meant, therefore, that in a free republic the leaders and a majority of the people are committed to doing what's best for the nation as a whole. When that commitment breaks down, when the people consider only their own personal well-being, they can no longer be depended upon to behave in the best interests of their nation. The result is laws, regulations, red tape and controls—things designed to force people

Excerpted from "Living Up to a Code of Ethics," speech given by Sanford N. McDonnell before the 21st Annual College Symposium on Ethical Issues and Decision Making, Hilton Head Island, SC, November 5, 1998. Reprinted with permission.

to be trustworthy. And these are instruments of bondage, not freedom.

Benjamin Franklin underlined this concept of Montesquieu's when he said, "Only a virtuous people are capable of freedom."

Traditional American Values

Throughout most of our history, certain basic, ethical values were considered fundamental to the character of the nation and to the people who made up the nation. These values were passed on from generation to generation in the home, the school and the religious institution—each one undergirding and reinforcing the others. We had a consensus not only on values but on the importance of those values; and from that consensus, we knew who we were as a people and where we were going as a nation.

In 1831 Alexis de Tocqueville came to this country to find out what it was that made this upstart, new nation so progressive and prosperous. He traveled all over the country and talked to people of all walks of life, and then went back to France and in 1835 published his classic *Democracy in America*. Incidentally, de Tocqueville hated slavery and considered the true America to be the northern, free states. In that context he wrote, "America is great because she is good, but if America ever ceases to be good America will cease to be great."

Today in America we have far too many twelve-year-olds pushing drugs, fourteen-year-olds having babies, sixteen-year-olds killing each other, and kids of all ages admitting to lying, cheating and stealing at epidemic numbers. We have crime and violence everywhere, unethical behavior in business, the professions

> *"If you [teach] kids . . . to really care about others they feel better about themselves and they work harder."*

and in government. In other words, we have a crisis of character all across America that is threatening to destroy the goodness which, as de Tocqueville put it, is the very foundation of our greatness. That is the bad news, but the good news is that we know what to do about it. And that is getting back to the core values of our American heritage in our homes, our schools, our businesses, our government and indeed in each of our daily lives. Ideally our young should be getting good character training in the home, but this is happening in far too few homes these days.

So it is in the schools that we have the greatest potential for overcoming the crisis of character that is raging all around us.

Character Education Programs

When our country was founded, Harvard, Yale and Princeton were already in existence as theological seminaries whose whole thrust was teaching the values of our Judeo-Christian faith. And from kindergarten through the university level, character education was considered just as important as intellectual knowledge. For many reasons, formal character education has been largely removed from the public schools. While we can't teach religion in the public schools anymore, we can teach the universal values common to all the great religions. With that conviction, in 1988 in seven of our public school districts, we in St. Louis formed a business education-community partnership and initiated a character education program called PREP, which stands for Personal Responsibility Education Process. It has now grown to thirty-four public school districts representing 426 individual schools with almost 250,000 students. They are not all getting the process, because it is still in a development mode in many of the districts. But where PREP has been implemented properly, it has produced very encouraging and sometimes dramatic results. Not only have behavior problems gone down, but one of the most exciting results is that academic performance has gone up. It is obvious that if you don't have law and order in the classrooms the teachers won't be able to teach anything. It is not so obvious but equally true that if you create a moral and caring community environment in the schools by teaching kids, for example, to really care about others they feel better about themselves and they work harder. The teachers are happier, the students are happier, the parents are happier, and the community is happier. It is a win-win program. Character education should be an integral part of the entire formal education system from kindergarten through graduate school.

> *"Character education should be an integral part of the entire formal education system from kindergarten through graduate school."*

From that background, I became a charter member and chairman of a nonprofit organization incorporated in Washington, D.C., called The Character Education Partnership, which is dedicated to promoting character education and to helping communities and cities throughout the country set up character education programs K–12 in their public schools.

The Character Education Partnership defines character, good character, as "understanding, caring about and acting on core ethical values such as honesty, responsibility, respect, kindness and caring for others." Prof. Kevin Ryan, a member of the board of directors of The Character Education Partnership, has a simpler definition of character, which is "knowing the good, loving the good and doing the good." In other words, building good character must involve the cognitive, the emotional and the physical—the head, the heart, the hand. As Aristotle put it: virtues are not mere thoughts but habits we develop by performing virtuous actions. We become kind by doing kind deeds. We become self-controlled by exercising self-control. Therefore, parents and educators should seek to help students to perform honest, kind, courteous, responsible, and self-disciplined acts over and over again until they become ingrained habits. That is character education. Developing character in this comprehensive sense requires a comprehensive educational approach—one that uses all aspects of schooling (academic subject matter, the instructional process, the management of the school environment) as opportunities for character development.

Essential Characteristics

What are some of the essential characteristics of a successful character education program?

First and foremost, the teachers must be role models. They must be caregivers and they must be moral people.

Second, the teachers and the parents in each school or district must come to consensus on what values they want the students in the school to learn and what those values mean. When this process is worked through, the school community has ownership and no one can criticize the values chosen, because everyone in the community has had the opportunity to participate.

Third, in the classroom teachers must teach the school values through the curriculum and in every other possible way, and the students should be encouraged to engage in moral reflection through reading, writing, and discussion.

Fourth, students should be involved in deciding the rules and their enforcement that they feel will make their classroom a good place in which to be and in which to learn. In other words, a micro, civil and democratic society is created in the classroom. When students help establish the rules they have ownership, and they use peer pressure to help the teacher keep order and discipline in the classroom.

Fifth, teachers should practice moral discipline, using the creation and enforcement of the rules as opportunities to foster moral reasoning and respect for others.

Sixth, cooperative learning should be used to teach kids how to help each other learn and how to work together. And, certainly, students should be taught how to resolve conflict in fair and nonviolent ways. And beyond the classroom the principal and her staff should use the total school environment to support and reinforce the values taught in the classroom. For example, service projects in the school and the community help students learn to care by giving care. One of the potentially most powerful activities in school and college is team sports, because it naturally involves the head, the heart, the hand. Coaches have the opportunity over

> *"Teachers must teach the school values through the curriculum and in every other possible way."*

and over again in team practice and competition to insist on teamwork, perseverance, hard work, honesty, responsibility, respect, caring, personal sacrifice for the team and good sportsmanship—all the basic values that make up a person of good character. If coaches emphasize that these values are important both on and off the playing field, they can be a tremendous help in building character. Then these athletes will be good role models for those young people who are not on the team and indeed for everyone old and young alike who watch them play and follow their behavior off the competitive field as well. . . .

Last but not least, the parents, the religious institutions, the businesses, and indeed the entire adult community should be recruited as partners in character education.

Positive Results

Let me give you a couple of examples of public schools that have had spectacular results with their character education programs. First, the Allen Elementary School in Dayton, Ohio, an inner city school with 60% of its students coming from single-parent homes and 70% from families on welfare was a near disaster in 1989. Allen was ranked 28th of Dayton's 33 elementary schools in test scores, and teachers couldn't teach because of the constant discipline problems. Principal Rudy Bernardo implemented a comprehensive character education program, and five years later Allen was number 1 in test scores and its behavior problems had improved dramatically.

> *"Above all, we believe the school itself must embody character."*

Secondly, the Jefferson Junior High School, an inner-city school in Washington, D.C., with approximately 800 Afro-American students, was having serious problems with drugs, student pregnancies and discipline. With a comprehensive character education program, Principal Vera White completely turned the school around over a five-year period. There have been almost no student pregnancies in the past few years, and Jefferson has been recognized for having the highest academic achievement in the city. The school now has a waiting list of more than 400 students.

Above all, we believe the school itself must embody character. It must be a moral community that helps students form caring attachments to adults and to each other, because these are the relationships that nurture both the desire to be a good person and the desire to learn.

The Importance of Character Education

Character without knowledge is weak and feeble, but knowledge without character is dangerous and a potential menace to society. Today's America won't achieve the goodness celebrated by de Tocqueville if we graduate young people from our schools who are brilliant but dishonest, who have great intellectual knowledge but don't really care about others, who are great thinkers but are irresponsible.

America can achieve both the goodness and greatness of de Tocqueville if we teach our young to do what is right, to tell the truth, to serve others, to work hard, when hardship comes to have courage, when you fail to try again, and to never ever give up.

Character education is one of the most important, if not the most important, answers to our national crisis of character and it is absolutely essential to any truly effective education reform movement. We know what to do. We are doing it in many parts of the nation, but we need to get on with character education as fast as possible in every school in America.

George Washington once said, "To personally understand and maintain the American way of life, to honor it by his own exemplary conduct, and to pass it intact to future generations is the responsibility of every true American." Let each one of us decide how we are going to discharge that responsibility to these great United States of America.

Character Education Programs Do Not Teach Students Ethical Behavior

by Alfie Kohn

About the author: *Alfie Kohn writes and lectures widely on education and human behavior. His books include* Punished by Rewards *and* Beyond Discipline: From Compliance to Community.

What goes by the name of character education nowadays is, for the most part, a collection of exhortations and extrinsic inducements designed to make children work harder and do what they're told. Even when other values are also promoted—caring or fairness, say—the preferred method of instruction is tantamount to indoctrination. The point is to drill students in specific behaviors rather than to engage them in deep, critical reflection about certain ways of being. This is the impression one gets from reading articles and books by contemporary proponents of character education as well as the curriculum materials sold by the leading national programs. The impression is only strengthened by visiting schools that have been singled out for their commitment to character education. . . .

Dubious Strategies

Some of the most popular schoolwide strategies for improving students' character seem dubious on their face. When President Bill Clinton mentioned the importance of character education in his 1996 State of the Union address, the only specific practice he recommended was requiring students to wear uniforms. The premises here are first, that children's character can be improved by forcing them to dress alike, and second, that if adults object to students' clothing, the best solution is not to invite them to reflect together about how this problem might be solved, but instead to compel them all to wear the same thing.

A second strategy, also consistent with the dominant philosophy of character education, is an exercise that might be called "If It's Tuesday, This Must Be Honesty." Here, one value after another is targeted, with each assigned its own day, week, or month. This seriatim approach is unlikely to result in a lasting commitment to any of these values, much less a feeling for how they may be related. Nevertheless, such programs are taken very seriously by some of the same people who are quick to dismiss other educational programs, such as those intended to promote self-esteem, as silly and ineffective.

Then there is the strategy of offering students rewards when they are "caught" being good, an approach favored by right-wing religious groups and orthodox behaviorists but also by leaders of—and curriculum suppliers for—the character education movement. Because of its popularity and because a sizable body of psychological evidence germane to the topic is available, it is worth lingering on this particular practice for a moment.

In general terms, what the evidence suggests is this: the more we reward people for doing something, the more likely they are to lose interest in whatever they had to do to get the reward. Extrinsic motivation, in other words, is not only quite different from intrinsic motivation but actually tends to erode it. This effect has been demonstrated under many different circumstances and with respect to many different attitudes and behaviors. Most relevant to character education is a series of studies showing that individuals who have been rewarded for doing something nice become less likely to think of themselves as caring or helpful people and more likely to attribute their behavior to the reward.

"Extrinsic incentives can, by undermining self-perceived altruism, decrease intrinsic motivation to help others," one group of researchers concluded on the basis of several studies. "A person's kindness, it seems, cannot be bought." The same applies to a person's sense of responsibility, fairness, perseverance, and so on. The lesson a child learns from Skinnerian tactics is that the point of being good is to get rewards. No wonder researchers have found that children who are frequently rewarded—or, in another study, children who receive positive reinforcement for caring, sharing, and helping—are less likely than other children to keep doing those things.

In short, it makes no sense to dangle goodies in front of children for being virtuous. But even worse than rewards are awards—certificates, plaques, trophies, and other tokens of

> *"[Character education programs] drill students in specific behaviors rather than . . . engage them in deep, critical reflection."*

recognition whose numbers have been artificially limited so only a few can get them. When some children are singled out as "winners," the central message that every child learns is this: "Other people are potential obstacles to my success." Thus the likely result of making students beat out their peers for the distinction of being the most virtuous is not only less intrinsic commitment to virtue but also a disruption of relationships and, ironically, of the experience of community that is so vital to the development of children's character.

Fundamental Problems

Unhappily, the problems with character education (in the narrow sense, which is how I'll be using the term unless otherwise indicated) are not restricted to such strategies as enforcing sartorial uniformity, scheduling a value of the week, or offering students a "doggie biscuit" for being good. More deeply troubling are the fundamental assumptions, both explicit and implicit, that inform character education programs. Let us consider five basic questions that might be asked of any such program: At what level are problems addressed? What is the underlying theory of human nature? What is the ultimate goal? Which values are promoted? And finally, How is learning thought to take place?

1. At what level are problems addressed? One of the major purveyors of materials in this field, the Jefferson Center for Character Education in Pasadena, California, has produced a video that begins with some arresting images—quite literally. Young people are shown being led away in handcuffs, the point being that crime can be explained on the basis of an "erosion of American core values," as the narrator intones ominously. The idea that social problems can be explained by the fact that traditional virtues are no longer taken seriously is offered by many proponents of character education as though it were just plain common sense.

> *"This . . . approach is unlikely to result in a lasting commitment to any of these values."*

But if people steal or rape or kill solely because they possess bad values—that is, because of their personal characteristics—the implication is that political and economic realities are irrelevant and need not be addressed. Never mind staggering levels of unemployment in the inner cities or a system in which more and more of the nation's wealth is concentrated in fewer and fewer hands; just place the blame on individuals whose characters are deficient. A key tenet of the "Character Counts!" Coalition, which bills itself as a nonpartisan umbrella group devoid of any political agenda, is the highly debatable proposition that "negative social influences can [be] and usually are overcome by the exercise of free will and character." What is presented as common sense is, in fact, conservative ideology.

Let's put politics aside, though. If a program proceeds by trying to "fix the kids"—as do almost all brands of character education—it ignores the accumulated evidence from the field of social psychology demonstrating that much of how we act and who we are reflects the situations in which we find ourselves. Virtually all the landmark studies in this discipline have been variations on this theme. Set up children in an extended team competition at summer camp and you will elicit unprecedented levels of aggression. Assign adults to the roles of prisoners or guards in a mock jail, and they will start to become their roles. Move people to a small town, and they will be more likely to rescue a stranger in need. In fact, so common is the tendency to attribute to an individual's personality or character what is actually a function of the social environment that social psychologists have dubbed this the "fundamental attribution error."

"Children who receive positive reinforcement for caring, sharing, and helping are less likely than other children to keep doing those things."

A similar lesson comes to us from the movement concerned with Total Quality Management associated with the ideas of the late W. Edwards Deming. At the heart of Deming's teaching is the notion that the "system" of an organization largely determines the results. The problems experienced in a corporation, therefore, are almost always due to systemic flaws rather than to a lack of effort or ability on the part of individuals in that organization. Thus, if we are troubled by the way students are acting, Deming, along with most social psychologists, would presumably have us transform the structure of the classroom rather than try to remake the students themselves—precisely the opposite of the character education approach.

A Dark View of Human Nature

2. What is the view of human nature? Character education's "fix-the-kids" orientation follows logically from the belief that kids need fixing. Indeed, the movement seems to be driven by a stunningly dark view of children—and, for that matter, of people in general. A "comprehensive approach [to character education] is based on a somewhat dim view of human nature," acknowledges William Kilpatrick, whose book *Why Johnny Can't Tell Right from Wrong* contains such assertions as: "Most behavior problems are the result of sheer 'willfulness' on the part of children."

Despite—or more likely because of—statements like that, Kilpatrick has frequently been invited to speak at character education conferences. But that shouldn't be surprising in light of how many prominent proponents of character education share his views. Edward Wynne says his own work is grounded in a tradition of thought that takes a "somewhat pessimistic view of human nature." The idea of character development "sees children as self-centered," in the opinion of Kevin Ryan, who directs the Center for the Advancement of Ethics and Character at Boston University as well as heading up the character education network of the Association for Supervision and Curriculum Development. Yet another writer approvingly traces the whole field back to the bleak world view of Thomas Hobbes: it is "an obvious assumption of character education," writes Louis Goldman, that people lack the instinct to work together. Without laws to compel us to get along, "our natural egoism would lead us into 'a condition of warre one against another.'" This sentiment is echoed by F. Washington Jarvis, headmaster of the Roxbury Latin School in Boston, one of Ryan's favorite examples of what character education should look like in practice. Jarvis sees human nature as "mean, nasty, brutish, selfish, and capable of great cruelty and meanness. We have to hold a mirror up to the students and say, 'This is who you are. Stop it.'"

Even when proponents of character education don't express such sentiments explicitly, they give themselves away by framing their mission as a campaign for self-control. Amitai Etzioni, for example, does not merely include this attribute on a list of good character traits; he *defines* character principally in terms of the capacity "to control impulses and defer gratification." This is noteworthy because the virtue of self-restraint—or at least the decision to give special emphasis to it—has historically been preached by those, from St. Augustine to the present, who see people as basically sinful.

In fact, at least three assumptions seem to be at work when the need for self-control is stressed: first, that we are all at war not only with others but with ourselves, torn between our desires and our reason (or social norms); second, that these desires are fundamentally selfish, aggressive, or otherwise unpleasant; and third, that these desires are very strong, constantly threatening to overpower us if we don't rein them in. Collectively, these statements describe religious dogma, not scientific fact. Indeed, the evidence from several disciplines converges to cast doubt on this sour view of human beings and, instead, supports the idea that it is as "natural" for children to help as to hurt. I will not rehearse that evidence here, partly because I have done so elsewhere at some length. Suffice it to say that even the most hard-headed empiricist might well conclude that the promotion of prosocial values consists to some extent of supporting (rather than restraining or controlling) many facets of the self. Any educator who adopts this more balanced position might think twice before joining an educational movement that is finally inseparable from the doctrine of original sin.

Promoting a Conservative Agenda

3. What is the ultimate goal? It may seem odd even to inquire about someone's reasons for trying to improve children's character. But it is worth mentioning that the whole enterprise—not merely the particular values that are favored—is often animated by a profoundly conservative, if not reactionary, agenda. Character education based on "acculturating students to conventional norms of 'good' behavior . . . resonates with neoconservative concerns for social stability," observed David Purpel. The movement has been described by another critic [Alan L. Lockwood] as a "yearning for some halcyon days of moral niceties and social tranquillity." But it is not merely a *social* order that some are anxious to preserve (or recover): character education is vital, according to one vocal proponent [Kevin Walsh], because "the development of character is the backbone of the economic system" now in place.

Character education, or any kind of education, would look very different if we began with other objectives—if, for example, we were principally concerned with helping children become active participants in a democratic society (or agents for transforming a society *into* one that is authentically democratic). It would look different if our top priority were to help students develop into

> *"The [character education] movement seems to be driven by a stunningly dark view of children."*

principled and caring members of a community or advocates for social justice. To be sure, these objectives are not inconsistent with the desire to preserve certain traditions, but the point would then be to help children decide which traditions are worth preserving and why, based on these other considerations. That is not at all the same as endorsing anything that is traditional or making the preservation of tradition our primary concern. In short, we want to ask character education proponents what goals they emphasize—and ponder whether their broad vision is compatible with our own.

4. Which values? Should we allow values to be taught in school? The question is about as sensible as asking whether our bodies should be allowed to contain bacteria. Just as humans are teeming with microorganisms, so schools are teeming with values. We can't see the former because they're too small; we don't notice the latter because they're too similar to the values of the culture at large. Whether or not we deliberately adopt a character or moral education program, we are always teaching values. Even people who insist that they are opposed to values in school usually mean that they are opposed to values other than their own.

And that raises the inevitable question: Which values, or whose, should we teach? It has already become a cliché to reply that this question should not trouble us because, while there may be disagreement on certain issues, such as abortion, all of us can agree on a list of basic values that children ought to have. Therefore, schools can vigorously and unapologetically set about teaching all of those values.

Teaching Controversial Values

But not so fast. Look at the way character education programs have been designed and you will discover, alongside such unobjectionable items as "fairness" or "honesty," an emphasis on values that are, again, distinctly conservative—and, to that extent, potentially controversial. To begin with, the famous Protestant work ethic is prominent: children should learn to "work hard and complete their tasks well and promptly, even when they do not want to," says Ryan. Here the Latin question *Cui bono?* comes to mind. Who benefits when people are trained not to question the value of what they have been told to do but simply to toil away at it—and to regard this as virtuous? Similarly, when Wynne defines the moral individual as someone who is not only honest but also "diligent, obedient, and patriotic," readers may find themselves wondering whether these traits really qualify as *moral*—as well as reflecting on the virtues that are missing from this list.

Character education curricula also stress the importance of things like "respect," "responsibility," and "citizenship." But these are slippery terms, frequently used as euphemisms for uncritical deference to authority. Under the headline "The Return of the 'Fourth R'"—referring to "respect, responsibility, or rules"—*U.S. News & World Report* recently described the growing popularity of such practices as requiring uniforms, paddling disobedient students, rewarding those who are compliant, and "throwing disruptive kids out of the classroom." Indeed, William Glasser observed some time ago that many educators "teach thoughtless conformity to school rules and call the conforming child 'responsible.'" I once taught at a high school where the principal frequently exhorted students to "take responsibility." By this he meant specifically that they should turn in their friends who used drugs.

Exhorting students to be "respectful" or rewarding them if they are caught being "good" may likewise mean nothing more than getting them to do whatever the adults demand. Following a lengthy article about character education in the *New York Times Magazine,* a reader mused, "Do you suppose that if Germany had had character education at the time, it would have encouraged children to fight Nazism or to support it?" The more time I spend in schools that are enthusiastically implementing character education programs, the more I am haunted by that question. . . .

> *"Character education programs [emphasize] values that are . . . distinctly conservative [and] potentially controversial."*

An Ineffective Teaching Style

5. What is the theory of learning? We come now to what may be the most significant, and yet the least remarked on, feature of character education: the way values are taught and the way learning is thought to take place.

The character education coordinator for the small Chicago elementary school also teaches second grade. In her classroom, where one boy has been forced to sit by himself for the last two weeks ("He's kind of pesty"), she is asking the children to define tolerance. When the teacher gets the specific answers she is fishing for, she exclaims. "Say that again" and writes down only those responses. Later comes the moral: "If somebody doesn't think the way you think, should you turn them off?" (No.)

Down the hall, the first-grade teacher is fishing for answers on a different subject. "When we play games, we try to understand the—what?" (Rules.) A moment later, the children scramble to get into place so she will pick them to tell a visitor their carefully rehearsed stories about conflict resolution. Almost every child's account, narrated with considerable prompting by the teacher, concerns name-calling or some other unpleasant incident that was "correctly" resolved by finding an adult. The teacher never asks the children how they felt about what happened or invites them to reflect on what else might have been done. She wraps up the activity by telling the children, "What we need to do all the time is clarify—make it clear—to the adult what you did."

The schools with character education programs that I have visited are engaged largely in exhortation and directed recitation. At first one might assume this is due to poor implementation of the programs on the part of individual educators. But the programs themselves—and the theorists who promote them—really do seem to regard teaching as a matter of telling and compelling. For example, the broad-based "Character Counts!" Coalition offers a framework of six core character traits and then asserts that "young people should be specifically and repeatedly told what is expected of them." The leading providers of curriculum materials walk teachers through highly structured lessons in which character-related concepts are described and then students are drilled until they can produce the right answers. . . .

Students are told what to think and do, not only by their teachers but by highly didactic stories, such as those in the Character Education Institute's "Happy Life" series, which end with characters saying things like "I am glad that I did not cheat," or "Next time I will be helpful," or "I will never be selfish again." Most character education programs also deliver homilies by way of posters and banners and murals displayed throughout the school. Children who do as they are told are presented with all manner of rewards, typically in front of their peers.

Does all of this amount to indoctrination? Absolutely, says Wynne, who declares that "school is and should and must be inherently indoctrinative." Even when character education proponents tiptoe around that word, their model of instruction is clear: good character and values are *instilled in* or *transmitted to* students. We are "planting the ideas of virtue, of good traits in the young," says William Bennett. The virtues or values in question are fully formed, and, in the minds of many character education proponents, divinely ordained. The children are—pick your favorite metaphor—so many passive receptacles to be filled, lumps of clay to be molded, pets to be trained, or computers to be programmed.

> *"[Character education programs] teach thoughtless conformity to school rules and call the conforming child 'responsible.'"*

Thus, when we see Citizen-of-the-Month certificates and "Be a good sport!" posters, when we find teachers assigning preachy stories and principals telling students what to wear, it is important that we understand what is going on. These techniques may appear merely innocuous or gimmicky; they may strike us as evidence of a scattershot, let's-try-anything approach. But the truth is that these are elements of a systematic pedagogical philosophy. They are manifestations of a model that sees children as objects to be manipulated rather than as learners to be engaged.

Ironically, some people who accept character education without a second thought are quite articulate about the bankruptcy of this model when it comes to teaching academic subjects. Plenty of teachers have abandoned the use of worksheets, textbooks, and

> *"Exhorting students to be 'respectful'... may... mean nothing more than getting them to do whatever the adults demand."*

lectures that fill children full of disconnected facts and skills. Plenty of administrators are working to create schools where students can actively construct meaning around scientific and historical and literary concepts. Plenty of educators, in short, realize that memorizing right answers and algorithms doesn't help anyone to arrive at a deep understanding of ideas.

And so we are left scratching our heads. Why would all these people, who know that the "transmission" model fails to facilitate intellectual development, uncritically accept the very same model to promote ethical development? How could they understand that mathematical truths cannot be shoved down students' throats but then participate in a program that essentially tries to shove moral truths down the same throats? In the case of individual educators, the simple answer may be that they missed the connection. Perhaps they just failed to recognize that "a classroom cannot foster the development of autonomy in the intellectual realm while suppressing it in the social and moral realms," as Constance Kamii and her colleagues put it not long ago.

In the case of the proponents of character education, I believe the answer to this riddle is quite different. The reason they are promoting techniques that seem strikingly ineffective at fostering autonomy or ethical development is that, as a rule, they are not *trying* to foster autonomy or ethical development. The goal is not to support or facilitate children's social and moral growth, but simply to "demand good behavior from students," in Ryan's words. The idea is to get compliance, to *make* children act the way we want them to.

Indeed, if these are the goals, then the methods make perfect sense—the lectures and pseudo-discussions, the slogans and the stories that conk students on the head with their morals. David Brooks, who heads the Jefferson Center for Character Education, frankly states, "We're in the advertising business." The way you get people to do something, whether it's buying Rice Krispies or becoming trustworthy, is to "encourage conformity through repeated messages." The idea of selling virtues like cereal nearly reaches the point of self-parody in the Jefferson Center's curriculum, which includes the following activity: "There's a new product on the market! It's Considerate Cereal. Eating it can make a person more considerate. Design a label for the box. Tell why someone should buy and eat this cereal. Then list the ingredients."

If "repeated messages" don't work, then you simply force students to conform: "Sometimes compulsion is what is needed to get a habit started," says William Kilpatrick. We may recoil from the word "compulsion," but it is the premise of that sentence that really ought to give us pause. When education is construed as the process of inculcating *habits*—which is to say, unreflective actions—then it scarcely deserves to be called education at all. It is really, as Alan Lockwood saw, an attempt to get "mindless conformity to externally imposed standards of conduct."

Notice how naturally this goal follows from a dark view of human nature. If you begin with the premise, as stated by Kilpatrick, that "good conduct is not our natural first choice," then the best you can hope for is "the development of good habits"—that is, a system that gets people to act unthinkingly in the manner that someone else has deemed appropriate. This connection became clear to Ann Medlock, whose Giraffe Project was designed to evoke "students' own courage and compassion" in thinking about altruism, but which, in some schools, was being turned into a traditional, authoritarian program in which students were simply told how to act and what to believe. Medlock recalls suddenly realizing what was going on with these educators: "Oh, *I* see where you're coming from. You believe kids are no damn good!"

The character education movement's emphasis on habit, then, is consistent with its view of children. Likewise, its process matches its product. The transmission model, along with the use of rewards and punishments to secure compliance, seems entirely appropriate if the values you are trying to transmit are things like obedience and loyalty and respect for authority. But this approach overlooks an important distinction between product and process. When we argue about which traits to emphasize—compassion or loyalty, cooperation or competition, skepticism or obedience—we are trafficking in value judgments. When we talk about how best to teach these things, however, we are being descriptive rather than just prescriptive. Even if you like the sort of virtues that appear in character education programs, and even if you regard the need to implement those virtues as urgent, the attempt to transmit or instill them dooms the project because that is just not consistent with the best theory and research on how people learn. . . .

The Need for Integration

I don't wish to be misunderstood. The techniques of character education may succeed in temporarily buying a particular behavior. But they are unlikely to leave children with a *commitment* to that behavior, a reason to continue acting that way in the future. You can turn out automatons who utter the desired words or maybe even "emit" (to use the curious verb favored by behaviorists) the desired actions. But the words and actions are unlikely to continue—much less transfer to new situations—because the child has not been invited to integrate them into his or her value structure. As John Dewey observed, "The required beliefs cannot be hammered in; the needed attitudes cannot be plastered on." Yet watch a character education lesson in any part of the country and you will almost surely be observing a strenuous exercise in hammering and plastering.

For traditional moralists, the constructivist approach is a waste of time. If values and traditions and the stories that embody them already exist, then surely "we don't have to reinvent the wheel," remarks Bennett. Likewise an exasperated Wynne: "Must each generation try to completely reinvent society?" The answer is no—and

> *"Children must be invited to . . . figure out for themselves . . . what kind of person one ought to be."*

yes. It is not as though everything that now exists must be discarded and entirely new values fashioned from scratch. But the process of learning does indeed require that meaning, ethical or otherwise, be actively invented and reinvented, from the inside out. It requires that children be given the opportunity to make sense of such concepts as fairness or courage, regardless of how long the concepts themselves have been around. Children must be invited to reflect on complex issues, to recast them in light of their own experiences and questions, to figure out for themselves—and with one another—what kind of person one ought to be, which traditions are worth keeping, and how to proceed when two basic values seem to be in conflict.

In this sense, reinvention is necessary if we want to help children become moral people, as opposed to people who merely do what they are told—or reflexively rebel against what they are told.

Studying Classic Literature Can Teach Students Ethics

by Christina Hoff Sommers

About the author: *Christina Hoff Sommers is a professor of philosophy at Clark University in Worcester, Massachusetts, and the W.H. Brady Fellow at the American Enterprise Institute in Washington, D.C. She is the editor of* Right and Wrong: Basic Readings in Ethics, *the coeditor of* Vice and Virtue in Every-day Life: Introductory Readings in Ethics, *and the author of* Who Stole Feminism? How Women Have Betrayed Women.

A lot is heard today about how Johnny can't read, can't write, and the trouble he has finding France on a map. It also is true that Johnny is having difficulty distinguishing right from wrong. Along with illiteracy and innumeracy, deep moral confusion must be added to the list of educational problems. Increasingly, today's young people know little or nothing about the Western moral tradition.

Moral Confusion

This was demonstrated by *Tonight Show* host Jay Leno, who frequently does "man-on-the-street" interviews. One night, he collared some young people to ask them questions about the Bible. "Can you name one of the Ten Commandments?," he asked two college-age women. One replied, "Freedom of speech?" Leno said to the other, "Complete this sentence: Let he who is without sin. . . ." Her response was "Have a good time?" Leno then turned to a young man and asked, "Who, according to the Bible, was eaten by a whale?" The confident answer was "Pinocchio."

As with many humorous anecdotes, the underlying reality is not funny at all. These young people are morally confused. They are the students I and other teachers of ethics see every day. Like most professors, I am acutely aware of the "hole in the moral ozone." One of the best things schools can do for America is to set about repairing it—by confronting the moral nihilism that is the norm for so many students.

Schools at all levels can do a lot to improve the moral climate of our society.

They can help restore civility and community if they commit themselves and have the courage to act.

When you have as many conversations with young people as I do, you come away both exhilarated and depressed. Still, there is a great deal of simple good-heartedness, instinctive fair-mindedness, and spontaneous generosity of spirit in them. Most of the students I meet are basically decent

> *"Today's young people know little or nothing about the Western moral tradition."*

individuals. They form wonderful friendships and seem to be considerate of and grateful to their parents—more so than the baby boomers were.

In many ways, they are more likeable than the baby boomers, being less fascinated with themselves and more able to laugh at their faults. A large number are doing volunteer work (70% of college students, according to one annual survey of freshmen). They donate blood to the Red Cross in record numbers and deliver food to housebound elderly people. They spend summer vacations working with deaf children or doing volunteer work in Mexico. This is a generation of youths that, despite relatively little moral guidance or religious training, is putting compassion into practice.

Living in a Moral Haze

Conceptually and culturally, though, today's young people live in a moral haze. Ask one of them if there are such things as "right" and "wrong," and suddenly you are confronted with a confused, tongue-tied, nervous, and insecure individual. The same person who works weekends for Meals on Wheels, who volunteers for a suicide prevention hotline or a domestic violence shelter, might tell you, "Well, there really is no such thing as right or wrong. It's kind of like whatever works best for the individual. Each person has to work it out for himself." The trouble is that this kind of answer, which is so common as to be typical, is no better than the moral philosophy of a sociopath.

I often meet students incapable of making even one single confident moral judgment, and the situation is getting worse. The things students say are more and more unhinged. Recently, several of my students objected to philosopher Immanuel Kant's principle of humanity—the doctrine that asserts the unique dignity and worth of every human life. They told me that, if they were faced with the choice between saving their pet or a human being, they would choose the former.

We have been thrown back into a moral Stone Age, wherein many young people are totally unaffected by thousands of years of moral experience and moral progress. The notion of objective moral truths is in disrepute, and this mistrust of objectivity has begun to spill over into other areas of knowledge. The concept of objective truth in science and history is being impugned as well. For example, an undergraduate at Williams College reported that her classmates, who had been taught that "all knowledge is a social construct," were doubtful that the Holocaust ever occurred. One of her classmates said, "Although the Holocaust may not have happened, it's a perfectly reasonable conceptual hallucination."

A creative writing teacher at Pasadena City College wrote an article in the *Chronicle of Higher Education* about what it is like to teach Shirley Jackson's famous short story "The Lottery" to today's college students. It is a tale of a small farming community that seems normal in every way, with people who are hardworking and friendly. As the plot progresses, however, the reader learns this village carries out an annual lottery in which the loser is stoned to death.

It is a shocking lesson about primitive rituals in a modern American setting. In the past, most students had understood "The Lottery" to be a warning about the dangers of mindless conformity, but now they merely think it is "Neat!" or "Cool!" They will not go out on a limb and take a stand against human sacrifice.

It was not always thus. When Thomas Jefferson wrote that all men have the right to life, liberty, and the pursuit of happiness, he did not say, "At least that is my opinion." He declared it as an objective truth. When suffragette Elizabeth Cady Stanton "amended" the Declaration of Independence by changing the phrase "all men" to "all men and women," she was not merely giving an opinion; she was insisting that females are endowed with the same rights and entitlements as males.

> *"I often meet students incapable of making even one single confident moral judgment."*

The assertions of Jefferson and Stanton were made in the same spirit—as self-evident truths, not personal judgments. Today's young people enjoy the fruits of the battles fought by such leaders, but they are not being given the intellectual and moral training to argue for and justify truth. In fact, the kind of education they are getting systematically is undermining their common sense about what is true and right.

Let me be concrete and specific: Men and women died courageously fighting the Nazis. They included American and Allied soldiers, as well as resistance fighters. Because brave people took risks to do what was right and necessary, Germany eventually was defeated. Today, with the assault on objective truth, many college students find themselves unable to say *why* the U.S. was on the right side in that war. Some even doubt that America *was* in the right. They are not even sure the salient events of World War II ever took place. They simply lack confidence in the objectivity of history.

Too many young people are morally confused, ill-informed, and adrift. This confusion gets worse, rather than better, once they go to college. If they are attending an elite school, they actually can lose their common sense and become clever and adroit intellectuals in the worst sense. Author George Orwell reputedly said, "Some ideas are so absurd that only an intellectual could believe them." The students of such intellectuals are in the same boat. Orwell did not know about the tenured radicals of the 1990s, but he was presciently aware that they were on the way.

The problem is not that young people are ignorant, distrustful, cruel, or treacherous. It is not that they are moral skeptics. They just talk that way. To put it bluntly, they are conceptually clueless. Students are suffering from "cognitive moral confusion."

The Great Relearning

What is to be done? How can their knowledge and understanding of moral history be improved? How can their confidence in the great moral ideals be restored? How can they be helped to become morally articulate, morally literate, and morally self-confident?

In the late 1960s, a group of hippies living in the Haight-Ashbury District of San Francisco decided that hygiene was a middle-class hang-up they could do without. So, they decided to live without it. Baths and showers, while not actually banned, were frowned upon. Essayist and novelist Tom Wolfe was intrigued by these hippies, who, he said, "sought nothing less than to sweep aside all codes and restraints of the past and start out from zero."

Before long, the hippies' aversion to modern hygiene had consequences that were as unpleasant as they were unforeseen. Wolfe describes them: "At the Haight-Ashbury Free Clinic there were doctors who were treating diseases no living doctor had ever encountered before, diseases that had disappeared so long ago they had never even picked up Latin names, such as the mange, the grunge, the itch, the twitch, the thrush, the scroff, the rot." The itching and the manginess eventually began to vex the hippies, leading them to seek help from the local free clinics. Step by step, they had to rediscover for themselves the rudiments of modern hygiene. Wolfe refers to this as the "Great Relearning."

The Great Relearning is what has to happen whenever earnest reformers extirpate too much. When, "starting from zero," they jettison basic social practices and institutions, abandon common routines, and defy common sense, reason, conventional wisdom—and, sometimes, sanity itself.

This was seen with the most politically extreme experiments of the 20th century—Marxism, Maoism, and fascism. Each movement had its share of zealots and social engineers who believed in starting from zero.

"The kind of education [students] are getting systematically is undermining their common sense about what is true and right."

They had faith in a new order and ruthlessly cast aside traditional arrangements. Among the unforeseen consequences were mass suffering and genocide. Russians and Eastern Europeans are beginning their own Great Relearning. They now realize, to their dismay, that starting from zero is a calamity and that the structural damage wrought by the political zealots has handicapped their societies for decades to come. They are learning that it is far easier to tear apart a social fabric than to piece one together again.

America, too, has had its share of revolutionary developments—not so much political as moral. We are living through a great experiment in "moral deregulation," an experiment whose first principle seems to be: "Conventional morality is oppressive." What is right is what works for us. We question everything. We casually, even gleefully, throw out old-fashioned customs and practices. Writer Oscar Wilde once said, "I can resist everything except temptation." Many in the 1960s generation made succumbing to temptation and license their philosophy of life.

> *"We must encourage and honor colleges that accept the responsibility of providing a classical moral education for their students."*

We jokingly call looters "non-traditional shoppers." Killers are described as "morally challenged"—again jokingly, but the truth behind the jests is that moral deregulation is the order of the day. We poke fun at our own society for its lack of moral clarity. In our own way, we are as down and out as those hippies knocking at the door of the free clinic.

Moral Conservationism

We need our own Great Relearning. Let me propose a few ideas on how we might carry out this relearning. The first, which could be called "moral conservationism," is based on this premise: We are born into a moral environment just as we are born into a natural environment. Just as there are basic environmental necessities—clean air, safe food, and fresh water—there are basic moral necessities. What is a society without civility, honesty, consideration, and self-discipline? Without a population educated to be civil, considerate, and respectful of one another, what will we end up with? The answer is, not much. For as long as philosophers and theologians have written about ethics, they have stressed the moral basics. We live in a moral environment. We must respect and protect it. We must acquaint our children with it. We must make them aware it is precious and fragile.

My suggestions for specific reforms are far from revolutionary and, indeed, some are pretty obvious. They are commonsense ideas, but we live in an age when common sense is increasingly hard to come by.

We must encourage and honor colleges that accept the responsibility of providing a classical moral education for their students. The last few decades of the 20th century have seen a steady erosion of knowledge and a steady increase in moral relativism. This is partly due to the diffidence of many teachers confused by all the talk about pluralism. Such teachers actually believe that it is wrong to "indoctrinate" our children in our own culture and moral tradition.

Of course, there are pressing moral issues around which there is no consensus. In a modern pluralistic society, there are arguments about all sorts of things. This is understandable. Moral dilemmas arise in every generation. Nevertheless, humanity long ago achieved consensus on many basic moral questions. Cheating, cowardice, and cruelty are wrong. As one pundit put it, "The Ten Commandments are not the Ten Highly Tentative Suggestions."

Teaching the Classics

While it is true that we must debate controversial issues, we must not forget there exists a core of noncontroversial ethical issues that were settled a long time ago. Teachers must make students aware there is a standard of ethical ideals that all civilizations worthy of the name have discovered. They must be encouraged to read the Bible, Aristotle's *Ethics,* William Shakespeare's *King Lear,* the Koran, and the *Analects* of Confucius. When they read almost any great work, they will encounter these basic moral values: integrity, respect for human life, self-control, honesty, courage, and self-sacrifice. All the world's major religions proffer some version of the Golden Rule, if only in its negative form: Do not do unto others as you would not have them do unto you.

The literary classics must be taught. The great books and great ideas must be brought back into the core of the curriculum. The best of political and cultural heritage must be transmitted. Author Franz Kafka once said that a great work of literature melts the "frozen sea within us." There are any number of works of art and philosophy that have the same effect.

> *"When [students] read almost any great work, they will encounter . . . basic moral values."*

American children have a right to their moral heritage. They should know the Bible. They should be familiar with the moral truths in the tragedies of Shakespeare and the political ideas of Jefferson, James Madison, and Abraham Lincoln. They should be exposed to the exquisite moral sensibility in the novels of Jane Austen, George Eliot, and Mark Twain, to mention some of my favorites. These great works are their birthright.

This is not to say that a good literary, artistic, and philosophical education suffices to create ethical human beings, nor to suggest that teaching the classics is all that is needed to repair the moral ozone. What is known is that we can not, in good conscience, allow America's children to remain morally illiterate. All healthy societies pass along their moral and cultural traditions to their children.

Support American Culture

This suggests another basic reform. Teachers, professors, and other social critics should be encouraged to moderate their attacks on our culture and its institutions. They should be encouraged to treat great literary works as literature and not as reactionary political tracts. In many classrooms today, students are encouraged to "uncover" the allegedly racist, sexist, and elitist elements in the great books.

Meanwhile, pundits, social critics, radical feminists, and other intellectuals on the cultural left never seem to tire of running down our society and its institutions and traditions. We are overrun by determined advocacy groups that overstate the weaknesses of our society and show very little appreciation for its merits and strengths.

> *"The great books and great ideas must be brought back into the core of the curriculum."*

I urge those professors and teachers who use their classrooms to disparage America to consider the possibility that they are doing more harm than good. Their goal may be to create sensitive, critical citizens, but what they actually are doing is producing confusion and cynicism. Their goal may be to improve students' awareness of the plight of exploited peoples, but they are producing individuals capable of doubting that the Holocaust actually took place and incapable of articulating moral objections to human sacrifice.

In my opinion, we are not unlike those confused, scrofulous hippies of the late 1960s who finally showed up at the doors of the free clinics in Haight-Ashbury to get their dose of traditional medicine. I hope we have the good sense to follow their example. We need to take an active stand against the divisive unlearning that is corrupting the integrity of our society.

Writer William Butler Yeats talked of the "center" and warned that it is not holding. Others talk of the threats to our social fabric and tradition. Nevertheless, we remain a sound society. We know how to dispel the moral confusion and get back our bearings and confidence. We have traditions and institutions of proven strength and efficacy, and we still are strong.

A Great Heritage of Ethics

We need to bring back the great books and the great ideas. We need to transmit the best of our political and cultural heritage. We need to refrain from cynical attacks against our traditions and institutions. We need to expose the folly of all the schemes for starting from zero. We need to teach our young people to understand, respect, and protect the institutions that protect us and preserve our free and democratic society.

If we do, when we engage in the Great Relearning that so badly is needed today, we will find that the lives of our morally enlightened children will be saner, safer, more dignified, and more humane.

Children Can Learn Ethics Through Hunting

by Michael Pearce

About the author: *A freelance writer based in Kansas, Michael Pearce contributes frequently to* Outdoor Life, Field and Stream, *and other hunting magazines. He is the author of three books about hunting and shooting.*

I talked with a boyhood friend a while back, a guy with whom I'd shared bass ponds and bobwhite hunts years ago. As is usual for thirtysomething parents, talk eventually turned to our children.

Spending Time with Kids

Like many parents, he was confused and concerned about his two teenagers. The word coming from school wasn't good, nor were relationships around the house. "Even when we're together, we're not really *together*," he said, admitting he was worried about the kids' lack of commitment, responsibility and respect. He eventually got around to the old cliché: "Kids these days. . . ."

When his complaining turned into pensive silence, I asked him a question for which I already knew the answer. "Are you getting into the field much these days?"

"No," he replied. "I've always wanted to get the boys out hunting, but I just haven't had the time." In that response, he summed up one of the reasons so many "kids these days" act the way they do. Much of the problem is "*parents* these days."

Whether it's because they're trying to run a household on their own or hustling to maintain a standard of living their parents never dreamed of, too many people spend far too little time with their children. The results are often attention-starved girls who end up mothers before they're out of their teens and latchkey kids with such low self-esteem they cave in to the slightest peer pressure.

For years, experts have said that time spent together doing anything, even simply working around the house, can strengthen family bonds and provide some direction. But I'm convinced that, when it comes to teaching lessons that

Reprinted from "Life Lessons," by Michael Pearce, *Outdoor Life,* December/January 1998. Reprinted with permission from the author.

will serve a child well throughout life, there's no better place than the outdoors, particularly the hunting fields.

Granted, I'm no psychologist with a 10-year study to back me up. Instead, I'm basing my assertions on 30-plus years of empirical evidence, watching young sportsmen and sportswomen grow into respectable adults. And as I watch my own children—13-year-old Lindsey and 10-year-old Jerrod—and the children of my hunting partners make use of lessons learned afield, I'm even more convinced that I'm right. Almost without exception, these young hunters are hard-working students who make full use of their natural abilities. Without fail, according to their teachers, these kids respect their elders and exhibit maturity that is years ahead of their peers.

Hard Work

No doubt the fact that these important lessons begin at such a young and impressionable age has an impact. Whereas most children these days get quick-fix gratification via television and video games, the child who is up before dawn and sent out into the cold darkness to help set up decoys quickly learns that the truly special things in life require effort and often a certain amount of discomfort. That lesson is only intensified when the youngster changes from tagalong partner to full-fledged hunter.

Before her first spring turkey hunt, Lindsey (then 11 years old) spent months getting ready, including hours at the range, trying various loads through her little 20-gauge. Together we watched every turkey video imaginable and went through countless full-camo dress rehearsals.

After three hard days of hunting, Lindsey finally connected on a well-earned, long-spurred Rio Grande. Trust me, Nintendo will never make a game that evokes such a glow of happiness and satisfaction. I'll never forget the joy she radiated when she called home that night, describing to Mom the miles we'd covered and the cactus needles we'd endured. Hopefully the kind of dedication Lindsey put into that Rio will translate into an ability to achieve goals that take years, rather than days—goals like college, a career and a well-planned family. On a more day-to-day level, the extra hour or so it takes to transform an essay from a B to an A will probably seem second nature to her.

> *"When it comes to teaching lessons that will serve a child well throughout life, there's no better place than the outdoors, particularly the hunting fields."*

Such feelings of accomplishment and pride benefit young hunters in other ways as well. Sociologists tell us one reason for the skyrocketing numbers of gang affiliations is the low self-esteem among America's youth. I've seen the pride in my son's eyes as he put a platter of barbecued goose—a bird he called, killed, cleaned and cooked—on the family dinner table. Having accomplished something wholly on his own, he knows that he can rely on himself.

Responsibility

While most American parents recoil in horror at the thought of their children using firearms, there's no question such exposure will have positive effects on the lives of young sportsmen and women. Those properly raised around guns develop a respect for safety early on that will no doubt spread to other aspects of their lives. There's no question that the child who is finally holding a loaded .22 at the range or a 20-gauge in the dove field knows that he or she is being trusted with something important and learns early on to shoulder responsibility.

These days gun-related deaths are as common as the fistfights of my youth, and too often a few minutes of passion lead to a lifetime of pain or even death. I take comfort in knowing that my children have pulled the trigger on game and held the lifeless consequences in their hands. What better way to learn that some acts, once committed, can never be undone?

Ethics

Of course it is possible to preach such values at home, and at one time or another most parents have, but you will be hard-pressed to find a better learning environment than the woods or marshes. Lecture your teen on ethics at the dinner table some night and you'll probably draw the typical puffy-cheeked, wide-eyed sigh of boredom and indifference. In the field, however, the student will be taking an active rather than a passive role, and the lesson will sink in.

In the spring of 1997, on our next-to-last turkey hunt, after several dry

> *"Almost without exception, these young hunters are hard-working students who . . . respect their elders and exhibit maturity that is years ahead of their peers."*

runs, Lindsey and I finally got a Rio Grande fired up in a remote section of sand hills. The bird double- or triple-gobbled at every call and came a quarter-mile at top speed.

But then the progress stopped. The tom was so close I could feel, as well as hear, the gobbles. Lindsey's breathing indicated her excitement. After a 10-minute stalemate, the tom slowly began moving away. We sneaked through the mixed cedars and cottonwoods and saw the reason for the turnaround—a brand-new, five-strand fence.

"Do we have permission for over there?" Lindsey asked.

"I don't think so," I replied. "It's a different landowner."

About that time the bird gobbled again.

"You know," I baited, looking her right in the eye, "all we'd have to do is cross the fence and slip a little ways into those woods, and we could call that bird right back—he's hot! Someone could sneak in, make the shot, run back to the fence and no one would ever know."

"Someone would know," Lindsey said after a few seconds of silence. "*We'd*

146

always know." With that she turned and headed away from the gobbler she wanted so badly. There's no way I could have better illustrated with words the importance of conscience and self-respect.

Family

Around the house teens often look upon parents as simple authority figures who stifle their activities or as ATMs that refuse to spit out enough money. But we can show our love and devotion much differently in the outdoors. Kids realize the sacrifice mom or dad makes when they leave their own guns at home while trying to call in a spring gobbler or by letting the child have his or her favorite opening day deer stand.

As children grow older, the outdoor relationship will become one of equality, giving the family a common ground to revert to when the generation gap begins to widen. At a time in my life when most fathers are watching their kids drift away, I can honestly say that my children and I are best friends.

Please don't think I'm so naive as to believe that we won't have our moments of parent-child strife. Hopefully, however, we'll still have our time afield, and if nothing else, their many memories will remind them that I am their friend.

As I write this, Jerrod and I are freshly back from his first big-game hunt—for pronghorns in New Mexico. The long-awaited trip was his reward for five years of hard work earning the rank of black belt in Tae Kwon Do. The boy spent time sighting-in his rifle, studying photographs of bucks and talking with experienced hunters.

Pronghorn hunts are supposed to be easy—one reason I chose the species for Jerrod's first big-game hunt—but this would be an exception. He had an excellent opportunity at a nice buck early the first morning but deferred to an older hunter who wasn't in nearly as good shape. On the second day, bucks always seemed to be just a few yards past his self-imposed shooting limit, and he refused to fire.

Last-minute successes on geese, turkeys, prairie chickens and doves have taught my kids the importance of persistence. Jerrod went into the third and final day full of optimism, and his faith never faded when a pair of coyotes ran off the herd or when he passed up a 125-yard chip shot at a nice buck because of the chance that the exiting bullet might strike a nearby doe.

> *"The child who is up before dawn . . . to help set up decoys quickly learns that the truly special things in life require effort."*

Finally, late that afternoon it looked like things were going his way when we found ourselves set up in front of a wandering herd of antelope. For more than an hour we sat in the sun and endured mosquitoes, biting ants and flies as we waited for the herd to crest a small rise. Eventually we could see the ebony horns of a buck just a few steps away from an easy shot. Jerrod's gun was up and the safety off, and only seconds separated him from a dream we'd shared for most of his life.

Then, in the blink of an eye it was over. The pronghorns busted and fled like a flushed covey of quail. Turning our heads, we saw a truckload of trespassers bearing down on the now long-gone antelope. I was crestfallen. I turned to Jerrod and apologized for things not going as I'd dreamed.

> *"Those properly raised around guns develop a respect for safety early on that will no doubt spread to other aspects of their lives."*

"That's okay, dad, you promised me a pronghorn hunt, not a pronghorn," he said with a smile. Then as he watched the truck of outlaws zoom from sight, he said, "I'd rather not fill a tag and know I did what was right."

It was I who had learned a tremendous amount about my son on that hunt. I know he's someone I can trust in the years to come, someone whom I'll always respect—and like as well as love. My dedication to helping him was never stronger.

And I remember thinking, "Kids these days. . . ."

Bibliography

Books

David Carr and Jan Steutel, eds.	*Virtue Ethics and Moral Education*. New York: Routledge, 1999.
Robert Coles	*The Moral Intelligence of Children: How to Raise a Moral Child*. New York: Plume, 1998.
Ron Cole-Turner, ed.	*Human Cloning: Religious Responses*. Louisville, KY: Westminster John Knox, 1997.
Barbara Cutney	*Challenges and Pleasures: Living Ethically in a Competitive World*. Lanham, MD: University Press of America, 1997.
Joseph L. Daleiden	*The Science of Morality: The Individual, Community, and Future Generations*. Amherst, NY: Prometheus Books, 1998.
Ralph Estes	*Tyranny of the Bottom Line: Why Corporations Make Good People Do Bad Things*. San Francisco: Berrett-Koehler, 1996.
David E.W. Fenner, ed.	*Ethics in Education*. New York: Garland, 1999.
Robert E. Frederick, ed.	*A Companion to Business Ethics*. Malden, MA: Blackwell, 1999.
Bernard Gert, Charles M. Culver, and K. Donner Clouser	*Bioethics: A Return to Fundamentals*. New York: Oxford University Press, 1997.
John Harris	*Clones, Genes, and Immortality: Ethics and the Genetic Revolution*. New York: Oxford University Press, 1998.
John W. Houck and Oliver F. Williams, eds.	*Is the Good Corporation Dead? Social Responsibility in a Global Economy*. Lanham, MD: Rowman & Littlefield, 1996.
Leon R. Kass and James Q. Wilson	*The Ethics of Human Cloning*. Washington, DC: AEI Press, 1998.
Helga Khuse and Peter Singer, eds.	*Bioethics: An Anthology*. Malden, MA: Blackwell, 1999.
David Lamb	*Organ Transplants and Ethics*. Brookfield, VT: Avebury, 1996.

Ethics

Jane Maienschein and Michael Ruse, eds.
Biology and the Foundation of Ethics. New York: Cambridge University Press, 1999.

Gilbert Meilaender
Bioethics: A Primer for Christians. Grand Rapids, MI: W.B. Eerdmans, 1996.

James Rachels
Can Ethics Provide Answers? and Other Essays in Moral Philosophy. Lanham, MD: Rowman & Littlefield, 1997.

J.B. Schneewind, ed.
Reason, Ethics, and Society. Peru, IL: Open Court, 1996.

Peter Singer
How Are We to Live? Ethics in an Age of Self-Interest. Amherst, NY: Prometheus Books, 1995.

Noel M. Tichy, Andrew R. McGill, and Lynda St. Clair, eds.
Corporate Global Citizenship: Doing Business in the Public Eye. San Francisco: New Lexington Press, 1997.

Frans de Waal
Good Natured: The Origins of Right and Wrong in Humans and Other Animals. Cambridge, MA: Harvard University Press, 1996.

Periodicals

Larry Arnhart
"Evolution and Ethics," *Books & Culture*, November/December 1999.

Paul F. Aspan
"Eye on Ethics," *America*, May 15, 1999.

Norman Augustine
"Reaping the Returns of Ethical Acts," *Vital Speeches of the Day*, August 15, 1997.

Bob Barr
"Situational Ethics," *Washington Times*, April 7, 1997.

Michael Barrier
"Doing the Right Thing," *Nation's Business*, March 1998.

N.E. Bowie
"Companies Are Discovering the Value of Ethics," *USA Today*, January 1998.

Myles Brand
"Lifting Up Our World: How Moral Values Affect the Way We Educate Our Young People," *Vital Speeches of the Day*, April 1, 1999.

Adam Bryant
"A Little Icing on Top," *Newsweek*, April 12, 1999.

William J. Byron
"Old Ethical Principles: The New Corporate Culture," *Vital Speeches of the Day*, July 1, 1999.

David R. Carlin Jr.
"Teaching Values in School," *Commonweal*, February 9, 1996.

Stephen L. Carter
"Becoming People of Integrity," *Christian Century*, March 13, 1996.

Denis P. Doyle
"Education and Character: A Conservative View," *Phi Delta Kappan*, February 1997.

Freeman Dyson
"Can Science Be Ethical?" *New York Review of Books*, April 10, 1997.

Mark P. Gibney
"Missing the Forest for the Trees," *Humanist*, May/June 1999.

Bibliography

George Johnson   "Ethical Fears Aside, Science Plunges On," *New York Times*, December 7, 1997.

John F. Kavanaugh   "The Burden of Ethics," *America*, October 11, 1997.

Thomas J. Lasley II   "The Missing Ingredient in Character Education," *Phi Delta Kappan*, April 1997.

Dave Masci   "The Cloning Controversy," *CQ Researcher*, May 9, 1997. Available from 1414 22nd St. NW, Washington, DC 20037.

R.A. McCormick   "Bioethics: A Moral Vacuum?" *America*, May 1, 1999.

Milton Moskowitz   "That's the Spirit," *Mother Jones*, July/August 1997.

Allan Sloan   "How Much Is Too Much?" *Newsweek*, March 17, 1997.

Herbert Stein   "Corporate America, Mind Your Own Business," *Wall Street Journal*, July 15, 1996.

Ron Taffel   "Teaching Values," *Parents*, October 1996.

Philip Yancey   "Dark Nature," *Books & Culture*, March/April 1998.

Organizations to Contact

The editors have compiled the following list of organizations concerned with the issues debated in this book. The descriptions are derived from materials provided by the organizations. All have publications or information available for interested readers. The list was compiled on the date of publication of the present volume; the information provided here may change. Be aware that many organizations take several weeks or longer to respond to inquiries, so allow as much time as possible.

American Medical Association (AMA)
515 N. State St., Chicago, IL 60610
(312) 464-5000
website: http://www.ama-assn.org

The AMA is the largest professional association for medical doctors. It helps set standards for medical education and practices, and it is a powerful lobby in Washington for physicians' interests. Its ethics division specializes in issues concerning medical ethics. The association publishes a number of medical journals, including the weekly publications *American Medical News* and *JAMA*.

Canadian Bioethics Society
Office of Medical Bioethics, University of Calgary, 3330 Hospital Dr. NW, Calgary, AB T2N 4N1, CANADA
(403) 220-7990 • fax: (403) 283-8524
e-mail: riddell@acs.ucalgary.ca • website: http://www.bioethics.ca

The society's membership consists of physicians, nurses, health care administrators, lawyers, theologians, philosophers, and others concerned with the ethical and humane dimensions of health care. It seeks to provide a forum for the exchange of views and ideas concerning bioethics, as well as assistance with the practical problems of decisions at the clinical, professional, and policy levels. The society publishes a triannual newsletter.

Canadian Centre for Ethics and Corporate Policy
50 Baldwin St., Toronto, ON M5T 1L4, CANADA
(416) 348-8691 • fax: (416) 348-8689
e-mail: ethicctr@interlog.com • website: http://www.ethicscentre.com

The center includes corporations and individuals dedicated to developing and maintaining an ethical corporate culture. It supports research into issues concerning corporate ethics and sponsors seminars, conferences, and lectures on business ethics. It publishes the bimonthly newsletter *Management Ethics*.

Center for Applied Christian Ethics (CACE)
Wheaton College, Wheaton, IL 60187
(630) 752-5886 • fax: (630) 752-5731
e-mail: cace@wheaton.edu • website: http://www.wheaton.edu/cace

CACE's goal is to raise moral awareness and elicit moral thinking by encouraging the application of Christian ethics to public policy and personal practice. The center sponsors conferences, workshops, and public debates on ethical issues. It produces a variety of resource materials, including cassettes, videotapes, the triannual newsletter *Discernment,* and the booklet "The Bible, Ethics, and Health Care: Theological Foundations for a Christian Perspective on Health Care."

The Center for Bioethics and Human Dignity
2065 Half Day Rd., Bannockburn, IL 60015
(847) 317-8180 • fax: (847) 317-8153
e-mail: cbhd@cbhd.org • website: http://www.bioethix.org

The center's mission is to bring Christian perspectives to bear on contemporary bioethical challenges facing individuals, families, communities, and society. It sponsors projects and conferences on such topics as euthanasia, genetic technology, and abortion. In addition, the center publishes books, cassettes, videotapes, multimedia packets, the biannual newsletter *Dignity,* and the journal *Ethics and Medicine.*

Center for Business Ethics (CBE)
Adamian Graduate Center, Room 108, Bentley College, Waltham, MA 02452
(781) 891-2981 • fax: (781) 891-2988
e-mail:cbeinfo@bentley.edu • website: http://ecampus.bentley.edu/dept/cbe/index.html

CBE is dedicated to promoting ethical business conduct in contemporary society. It helps corporations and other organizations strengthen their ethical cultures through educational programming and consulting. The center maintains a multimedia library and publishes the quarterly journal *Business and Society Review.* CBE also publishes a variety of books, including *Business Ethics: A Primer* and *Ethics Matters: How to Implement Values-Driven Management.*

Common Cause
1250 Connecticut Ave. NW, Suite 600, Washington, DC 20036
(202) 833-1200 • fax: (202) 659-3716
website: http://www.commoncause.org

Common Cause is a liberal lobbying organization that works to improve the ethical standards of Congress and government in general. Its priorities include campaign reform, making government officials accountable for their actions, and promoting civil rights for all citizens. The organization publishes the quarterly magazine *Common Cause* in addition to position papers and reports.

Ethics Resource Center
1747 Pennsylvania Ave. NW, Suite 400, Washington, DC 20006
(202) 737-2258 • fax: (202) 737-2227
e-mail: ethics@ethics.org • website: http://www.ethics.org

The center works to restore America's ethical foundations by fostering integrity, ethical conduct, and basic values in the nation's institutions. It also strives to create international coalitions dedicated to global ethics. The center supports character education and has developed several video-based learning programs for use in schools. Its publications include *Creating a Workable Company Code of Ethics, The Desktop Guide to Total Ethics Management,* and the quarterly newsletter *Ethics Today.*

The Hastings Center
Garrison, NY 10524-5555
(914) 424-4040 • fax: (914) 424-4545
e-mail: mail@thehastingscenter.org • website: http://www.thehastingscenter.org

Since its founding in 1969, the center has played a central role in responding to advances in medicine, the biological sciences, and the social sciences by raising ethical questions related to such advances. It conducts research on ethical issues and maintains a library of resources relating to ethics. The center publishes books, papers, guidelines, and the bimonthly *Hastings Center Report*.

Institute for Global Ethics

11 Main St., PO Box 563, Camden, ME 04843
(207) 236-6658 • fax: (207) 236-4014
e-mail: webethics@globalethics.org • website: http://www.globalethics.org

Dedicated to fostering global ethics, the institute focuses on ethical activities in education, the corporate sector, and public policy. It conducts ethics training seminars, sponsors lectures and workshops, develops curricular materials for elementary and secondary schools, and promotes community-based character education programs. Its publications include the quarterly newsletter *Insights on Global Ethics* and the books *How Good People Make Tough Choices: Resolving the Dilemmas of Ethical Living* and *Heartland Ethics: Voices from the American Midwest*.

Josephson Institute of Ethics

4640 Admiralty Way, Suite 1001, Marina del Rey, CA 90292-6610
(310) 306-1868 • fax: (310) 827-1864
website: http://www.josephsoninstitute.org

The institute's mission is to improve the ethical quality of society by advocating principled reasoning and ethical decision making. It offers Ethics in the Workplace training seminars as well as specialized consulting services for businesses. Its Character Counts! coalition promotes character education through the partnership of educational and human-service organizations. The institute publishes the book *Good Ideas to Help Young People Develop Good Character*, the booklet "Making Ethical Decisions," and the videotapes *Kids for Character* and *Choices Count!*

Kennedy Institute of Ethics

Georgetown University, Box 571212, Washington, DC 20057-1212
(202) 687-8099 • fax: (202) 687-8089
e-mail: kicourse@gunet.georgetown.edu
website: http://www.georgetown.edu/research/kie

The institute is a teaching and research center that offers ethical perspectives on major policy issues in the fields of medicine, religion, law, journalism, international affairs, and business. It houses the National Reference Center for Bioethics Literature, produces an on-line medical ethics database, and conducts regular seminars and courses in bioethics. The institute's publications include the annual *Bibliography of Bioethics*, the quarterly *Kennedy Institute of Ethics Journal*, and the Scope Note Series on specific topics concerning biomedical ethics.

Park Ridge Center for the Study of Health, Faith, and Ethics

211 E. Ontario St., Suite 800, Chicago, IL 60611-3215
(312) 266-2222 • fax: (312) 266-6086

The center explores the relationships between health, faith, and ethics, focusing on the religious dimensions of illness and health. It seeks to help clergy, health care professionals, ethicists, educators, and public policymakers address ethical issues and create ethical policies. The center publishes the quarterly *Second Opinion*, the newsletter *Centerline*, and the book series Health and Medicine in the Faith Traditions.

Index

Index

Index